LAF with the Habits of Mind:
Strategies and Activities for Teaching Diverse Language Learners

Chapter 1
Introduction

This book is meant to give teachers of language learners the tools they need to create engaging, interactive and well-planned activities that promote both language acquisition and higher order thinking skills. Initial chapters will give an overview of what we know about language acquisition according to research, as well as considerations on how language and culture are interrelated. Since it is impossible to separate language from culture, we must look at these two sides of the same coin together. In addition, thinking is part of the language/culture connection. We use our language to think, we think about things that our culture presents to us as worthy of thought, and we express our thoughts with language. This book is an attempt to interweave the teaching of language to second language learners with the teaching of thinking grounded in the cultural context of the target language. This should be done while valuing the cultural perspectives and knowledge that learners bring to the classroom.

Throughout this book, I will tell you stories that help to highlight issues and considerations in the teaching and learning of languages. Storytelling is a way to deliver information that will stick in the mind of the reader or listener. Stories serve to teach in a way that is effective because they personalize information, they engage an emotional response that helps us retain information, and they even stimulate neurological pathways in the brain that promote empathy (Garmston, 2019).

All of these aspects of storytelling are essential for teachers of language learners to keep in mind. As teachers we are also learners, and, as demonstrated throughout this book, we can benefit greatly by using these concepts of storytelling in our own language classrooms. I will start with my own immigration and language learning story and show you how what I experienced as a child language learner and immigrant taught me valuable lessons for the language classroom. In addition to sharing our own stories of how we learn languages, we also need to become listeners of learner stories. By listening to our learners' stories, we can come to understand their particular needs in the language classroom and develop activities to meet those needs. In this way we can create empathetic, thoughtful and effective classroom environments where language learning can flourish.

Immigration and Language Acquisition: A Personal Story

When I think about what led to my becoming a teacher educator focusing on linguistic and cultural minority students, I feel that I must go way back. It is not enough to talk about my training as a teacher, or my travels around the world teaching English; I need to reach back into my own childhood as an immigrant and language learner. The linguistic and cultural experiences that I have accumulated over time have profoundly affected and informed my beliefs about teaching and learning. They have occasionally led me down dead-end paths where I had to backtrack and change direction, but they have more often allowed me to empathize with my own learners and understand the frustrations that accompany the journey from one way of knowing to another. Learning a language and becoming part of a new culture is more than an academic and social achievement, it is a change in identity and mindset. It is a change in the very essence of who we are.

I will share my immigration and language acquisition story with you. As you read, try to notice all of the advantages I had as a learner, as well as the disadvantages and challenges that I faced. The particular family situation that I came from, my first language literacy, my age at the time of immigration, the environment that I encountered and my own personality all contributed to the process of language acquisition that I went through. It is by looking back at my own experience and the many experiences of my students throughout the years, as well as reading and thinking about language acquisition theory and practice, that I have come up with my own checklist for what conditions are necessary to create Language Acquisition Friendly (LAF) activities. These activities all share certain characteristics that you will notice as you read my story and that you will see over and over again throughout this book. In a nutshell, a LAF activity is

- interactive;
- cooperative;
- personal and meaningful;
- engaging;
- encourages critical and creative thinking;
- embraces multiple perspectives;
- and uses the target language in purposeful ways.

Look for these elements in my own story and we will explore them and expand on them throughout the book.

A Reluctant Immigrant

I was born in Buenos Aires, Argentina at a time when most mothers did not work outside the home, and most children did not travel overseas. I was not like most people. My parents were both physicians, and by the time I was three years old, both of them at some point had left me behind in Argentina to live abroad in different countries. My father lived in England for a year doing a post doc, leaving me with my mother in Argentina. Following this, they both moved to the Netherlands for another post doc, leaving me with my adoring grandmothers. I suppose the move might have been a last-ditch attempt to save their marriage even as they gained important experience in cytology research. The marriage wasn't saved, and soon after they came back to Argentina, my mother left permanently to live in the United States. She took a job in Buffalo, New York, without any experience with the country or the language — or escalators or snow. She was offered a position there at a time when female doctors were few and far between in the United States, and immigrants with professional degrees were readily welcomed.

I remained in Buenos Aires with my father, grandparents, aunts and uncles, cousins and friends. I was comfortable and content in my home country where the language and the culture were familiar and the noises of the city lulled me to sleep at night. I was at home in a place I treasured, where the food was always delicious, and where the affection and attention for a semi-motherless four-year-old was constant and abundant. Despite all the comings and the goings of my parents, I was a happy child. I had an extensive vocabulary in Spanish, living in a highly literate household where my father wrote books and articles after his hospital shifts, and where he imparted to me a deep love for learning.

4

My eccentric father taught me to read when I was very young. He used his own method based on bad words and a set of wooden letter blocks. Since Spanish is a phonetic language and many 'bad' or 'bathroom words' are four letters long (caca, moco, pipi — and much worse), the bad word method is quite easy, entertaining, and effective. I later taught my own kids to read using the same method. Back then I lived happily in the middle of the city in a cozy apartment where my grandmother sang songs and told stories all day, while I drew pictures and read bad words spelled out with wooden blocks. I was very lucky.

Soon after my fourth birthday, I started preschool and loved it. My teacher, Señorita Susana, had a beautiful and welcoming smile. My best friend Julietta and I held hands and walked into school together every morning while my grandmother and Julietta's mother chatted and fussed over us, calling out reminders and blowing us kisses. We felt very grown up in our crisp white uniforms and patent leather shoes. I believe we took ourselves quite seriously and considered preschool a formidable academic challenge.

Julietta and I talked endlessly about everything, learned to paste things in our notebooks, and planned to be best friends for life. Little did we know that our friendship would soon come to an abrupt and permanent end. As I think back on those days, I sometimes wonder if I made Julietta up. No doubt she did exist, but maybe those conversations I recall, those moments together, were created by me as something to hold on to when I was alone, lonely, and far from my neighborhood preschool and everything that was ever familiar.

One day a few months in to the school year, my father surprised me with some exciting news. He told me that we would soon be traveling to the United States of America to visit my mother. She had left a year before, and I hardly remembered her. Of course I knew I had a mother, and I knew I loved my mother and that she loved me. If I ever had any doubt about that it is not something that I can remember. However, I hadn't seen or spoken with my mother for over a year (this was back in the day of the horrifyingly expensive overseas phone call and not yet developed Internet technologies), and at the age of four, a year is a very long time.

Although I don't remember many details of those first four years of my life in Argentina, I do remember quite a few details about the trip to the U.S. and the consequences of that trip. The most memorable travel story that was told and retold by my father for years was the attempted hijacking of our plane to Cuba on the way to New York. A short and sweaty brown-suited mentally ill man with a fake bomb caused us to have an unexpected layover in Venezuela, mostly notable because of the heat. The story of the hijacking grew a little bit more dangerous and exciting with each retelling, but the truth is that nothing of significance happened, except that it was the first time I heard my father speak English.

At some point during that long flight to New York City, I remember the pilot coming back to where we sat. He began speaking to my father using a language that was unintelligible to me. Apparently, they somehow knew my father was a doctor and wondered if he could help talk to the hijacker, who appeared to be more mentally unstable than dangerous. When the pilot came over I was worried because I didn't know who was flying the plane. The English sounded strange to me, and a little bit ridiculous, but the tin airplane wings and coloring book the English speaking flight attendant gave me were cool. Clearly, I decided, English was good for something.

The next most retold story about that first trip on a plane and to a new country was my reaction to the food at the airport in New York City. Apparently, we had to wait for a long time, maybe a whole day in New York since we had missed our original flight due to the strange hijacking attempt. With such a long wait, I became hungry and asked for food. My father was not familiar with the pastries he saw offered at the airport, so he decided to buy one of each for us to try. According to him, he put about five different delicious looking pastries in front of me, knowing I had a sweet tooth and a big appetite, and feeling sure that I would love at least one of them. I then proceeded to very meticulously take the absolute tiniest manageable crumb I could from each pastry in turn, sampling each one thoughtfully. When I was finished I bluntly declared that I did not like the food in the United States and would not be eating.

My father worried that I would refuse to eat in the United States and waste away to nothing. That certainly did not happen as I soon discovered chocolate chip cookies, peanut butter, and so many other wonderful things to eat that I have struggled to control my food consumption ever since. I wonder sometimes if I really didn't like the food that day, or if I even tasted it. Maybe I wanted to make my father suffer a little bit. Maybe I had a feeling that I was being dropped off thousands of miles from home, though nobody bothered to tell me that. Childhood immigrants often don't get a chance to say goodbye because they don't necessarily know that they are leaving forever.

When we finally arrived in Buffalo, New York, we were making our way through customs when my father told me to look up. There, behind a long row of windows overlooking the customs area (according to the picture in my mind), waited the families and loved ones of international passengers. In the middle of that group was a woman holding a stuffed bunny with a geometric pastel design on its tummy and two long, floppy ears. She was smiling and waving down to me. I couldn't wait to get to her and get my hands on that bunny. According to my mother, once I had passed customs I let go of my father's hand and ran over to her, gave her a big hug and kiss, thanked her for the bunny, hugged it tightly to me and started talking to her about my trip. She had been worried that I would be shy around her, or reject her after all the time that had passed, and was overjoyed and emotional when I was neither shy, nor resentful.

My mother used to tell me that she couldn't say a word when I reached for her hand. My easy acceptance of her was overwhelming and comforting. Evidently, I did enough talking for both of us. Separation of parents and children, sometimes for years at a time, is not uncommon among immigrant families and is often fraught with difficult consequences. Language barriers can develop, and a lack of connection or shared set of ways of knowing and understanding the world can ensue. Immigration can turn family into strangers and strangers into family, as I would soon discover.

My parents and I remembered and retold different parts of my immigration story. What was significant to them as adults was less meaningful to me, and I'm afraid that what I experienced as a child was completely unknown to them. The most important thing I can recall about moving to the U.S. is the profound sensation of loss I felt. Not only did I lose my country, my grandmother and my father, my extended family, my friends and my school, but I also lost my ability to communicate in the world of words. I could not express the loss I felt with the right vocabulary or grammar in a new language. There were no phone conversations to remind me of the sounds of my own language coming from the voices I loved. In short, I was a four-year-old reluctant immigrant that went through a period of several months during which I chose not to believe I had immigrated at all.

My parents were divorcing, but I didn't know that. After a week or so in the U.S., my father explained to me that he was going to work one day, and left. That evening, as I waited for him to return, my mother haltingly told me that he had returned to Argentina because his work was there. I did not believe her. I told her it was impossible that he would leave without me, and proceeded to pack my suitcase, grab my bunny, and wait for him by the door. I don't know how long I waited but eventually I fell asleep, waking up the next day with stuffed bunny still firmly clutched in my arms and no sign of my father. After the initial shock, I became very angry. I wanted nothing to do with the U.S., the English language or anything at all, and I showed it. In school, I cried all day unless allowed to set the table. I went to a private school that used actual plates, silverware and napkins at lunch each day. Maybe setting the table was comforting because it had been something I did in Argentina. I really don't know. Regardless, my penchant for setting tables did not last long.

In the mornings, when the school bus came to pick me up, my mother and the bus driver had to force me on as I kicked and screamed. I have a vague memory of this that still provokes a mixture of both frustration and shame. I wanted to go home to Argentina, but I couldn't. The language and culture were thrust upon me, and the only parent I really knew had abruptly left. I wonder how many kids go through similar experiences today. I wonder how many immigrant children carry the wounds of their immigration in their hearts and how that affects their learning process. In the grand scheme of things my experience was a cakewalk compared with the experiences of child refugees and other displaced persons due to war, famine or economic hardship. Yet, my immigration journey was extremely significant to me, and caused quite a bit of inner turmoil and confusion. Each of us carries our own complicated story, but some of us are hauling boulders while others are clutching pebbles.

I didn't see my father again for several years. By the time he came to visit me, I was a different person. It was no longer natural and easy between us. Immigration had changed me, and it changed our relationship to the very end. We no longer had one common language that was the most natural language for both of us. English had become my strongest language, and though he was a fluent English speaker, I could not bear to hear my father speak the language. He wanted to practice with me but I resisted. His speaking English probably seemed like another betrayal. Although I insisted that he speak Spanish with me, my own Spanish was not good enough to fully express myself. We were still father and daughter, full of all the love and complexity of such a relationship, but we were also strangers, separated by a language and a culture, and a hundred unspoken reproaches.

Despite many years and many visits, including very long stays in Argentina, my father and I could never again recapture the relationship we once had. The way we separated and the time apart, each living in a different cultural and linguistic milieu, worked as a kind of barrier between us. My father wrote me hundreds of letters over the years. The letters included newspaper clippings and footnotes, and covered a wide range of academic topics and historical oddities—anything he thought might capture my interest. Yet, he didn't say much about the things that truly interested me, such as my grandmother, my friends, my neighborhood, or the taste of pizza in Buenos Aires.

When my father and I got together, I couldn't ask him about why he had left me so abruptly, and why he hadn't insisted on my returning to Argentina every summer. Whenever I got near those subjects there was awkwardness and pain, and so I usually let it go. Often, when I asked too many questions that he didn't feel like answering, he would say to me (in English) "no personal questions," with a wry smile. His use of English, something he knew I strongly disliked, would effectively shut me up and end the line of inquiry he did not want to engage in. But if you can't ask your parent personal questions, who can you ask? Immigration can sometimes lead to a loss of the ability to communicate on a deeper level with even the closest family.

When I finished my Masters in TESOL in California, my father came to see me. It was somewhat uncomfortable, as many of our visits were. It usually took us a couple of weeks to warm up to each other, and even then it was awkward. One day I decided to push through the discomfort and insist that he explain how he could have left me at the age of four without letting me know he was leaving. I pushed further to know why he had not insisted that I go back every year, or why he had not come back to see me. My questions made him cry. I had ever seen an adult man cry. His tears shut me up quickly and forever. Sometimes, it seems, silence is the price we pay to maintain relationships made fragile by many years of separation and many years of regret. Silence is part of everyone's immigration story.

The linguistic and cultural learning experiences I had during my first years as a young immigrant have remained important to me throughout my entire life. I have no doubt that they led me in an indirect way to a career in TESOL and to a passion for helping others navigate new languages and cultures. But perhaps the most important thing that time and those experiences taught me was that language is an essential component of identity, and the ticket to determining our own destinies. I made sure to excel in English, and when I started to lose my Spanish, I worked hard to regain it. I became curious about culture and identity and decided to read as much as I could about it, to live it through travel and introspection, and eventually to share my ideas with others.

Another important lesson I have carried with me since the time when I first became an immigrant is the idea that kids are full-fledged people with the ability to feel, think, and problem solve as much as adults, even if not in the same ways or about the same issues. Even though children are in many senses powerless, they are already thinkers and dreamers from the earliest of ages. Even though I was only four years old, I know I could think critically and creatively in Spanish, to have strong opinions and emotions, and to know how to express those in my own language. Learning a new language was something I had not looked forward to. I was comfortable in my own world of words and navigating a new one was not my idea of a good time.

Before our trip, my father had hired an English teacher to come to the house a few times so that I could begin learning the language. I was not interested. I strongly resisted the idea of learning English and instead involved the teacher in drawing, playing dolls and having a 'tea party' with me in Spanish. I am sure that if the teacher had taken the opportunity to play with me while using English rather than trying to teach me decontextualized vocabulary, grammar and dialogues, I might have learned something and had fun in the process. This didn't happen. In those days, most teachers probably believed in a grammar and vocabulary memorization based approach, and I am sure that my English teacher had all the best intentions, yet none of the best strategies to reach a reluctant learner like me. Now we know better, though the best strategies are not always practiced.

Despite my reluctance and resistance, not uncommon in children who immigrate at a young age, I learned to communicate in English within a relatively short period of time. This is particularly true of those children who come from middle class and higher economic brackets, with well-educated parents who can provide them with many social and academic opportunities—children who are as lucky as I was.

My mother used to tell an anecdote about how quickly I learned the English language after I came to the United States. I arrived in May and began attending a very good school, followed by summer-long camp at the same school. There, I was surrounded by English through recreational activities for many hours a day. When kindergarten started in September, my mother sent me off to the same wonderful school. A few months into the school year, she went to a parent-teacher conference full of concern for my academic future and English language skills. Apparently, I wasn't very forthcoming about what went on during the school day, and she had never heard me speak anything other than Spanish. I'm sure I was still angry about having been unceremoniously dumped in a new country with a new parent, and was perhaps giving her something of a silent treatment.

After my kindergarten teacher talked to her about my small and large motor skills, my mother asked her if I understood what was going on in class. The teacher, confused, asked my mother what she meant. My mother repeated the question, wanting to know if I understood the teacher and the other children well enough to function. The teacher remained confused and asked my mother why she was worried that I might not understand. My mother replied that it was because I had just arrived in the country five months earlier and didn't speak English. According to my mother the teacher was dumbfounded. She had no idea that I was not a native English speaker just like all of the other children in the class.

My mother told this story many times. She saw it as an indication of my general brilliance and advanced linguistic abilities. She thought it meant that I had learned perfect English in just a few months. I thought so too, for many years, until I started studying TESOL. I soon realized that I had not actually learned English in just a few months. Rather, I had learned how to get by on a little bit of English, how to observe others carefully to understand what was going on, and, perhaps most importantly, I had started to play with other children.

Age, Environment & Teaching

I had immigrated into an ideal language-learning situation. I was in a good school with caring teachers who emphasized creative play. I spent many hours a day in an all-English environment where the primary expectation was to have fun, follow simple directions, participate in routines, and express myself artistically. There is probably no greater environment for language acquisition in school than a play-based preschool, and that is exactly where I ended up. The limited amount of language I had to speak was mostly personal, ritualistic and repetitive. I had another advantage that all small children have: the ability to pronounce new sounds and sound like a native speaker.

The facility of small children in pronunciation far exceeds the capabilities of older children and adults. The native sounding pronunciation often fools teachers and others into thinking that the kids understand everything, when in reality they don't. Although this becomes a problem when teachers don't realize that language learners need more scaffolds, repetition, and context clues because they overestimate their linguistic abilities, it is also a great advantage for young learners who are interacted with as if they understand everything. These learners are met with high expectations, asked critical thinking questions, and given challenging tasks. Because of the hands-on nature of the lower grades, this ability of kids to fool teachers with their pronunciation is ideal.

Language learners can figure out much of what is going on around them through observation and participation in common classroom rituals. As they arrive in a new linguistic and cultural context at higher grades, the context-embedded language of preschool and kindergarten starts to fade and the context-reduced language of the upper grades emerges. At the same time, there is increased pressure to perform in the new language rapidly, to take assessments in that language and to acculturate quickly. Whereas we give small children a chance to play, make many mistakes and explore in a language- and context-rich environment, we ask older children and adults to learn faster with less opportunity, and a less ideal environment to do so. Language acquisition is a long process that varies with individuals, their environments, and their interactions with native speakers. No matter where immigrants end up, language acquisition takes time, but the younger they arrive, the less time it seems to take. In addition, the younger the learners, the better the language acquisition environment most find themselves in.

As teachers of language learners, we can manipulate the environment of the classroom to enhance the opportunities for interaction, figuring out language, and negotiating meaning. When we move away from traditional approaches to language acquisition for older children and adults that concentrate heavily on grammar and vocabulary memorization, and towards more communicative, creative, and task-based interactive methods, we are giving our learners a better chance to succeed, and a more welcoming environment to succeed in.

In addition to modifying our general teaching strategies and methodologies to give our learners a more welcoming, interactive and positive language-learning experience, we must also encourage them to think critically and creatively. When learners are given opportunities to use higher-order thinking from the earliest ages they become good problem solvers. Often, although teachers know to question and stimulate the thinking of their mainstream students, they neglect to do this with second-language learners. The idea is that these learners must first learn the language, and later learn to think critically. However, this is a false assumption. Language learners can participate in language acquisition activities that are also critical and creative thinking activities from the very beginning levels, and when they do this they are more likely to remain engaged in lessons and to be motivated to continue learning.

I was extremely lucky to immigrate into a situation that encouraged me to play creatively even before I knew one word in the English language. The environment of my preschool included plenty of unstructured interaction with a variety of native speakers, and plenty of opportunities to make friends. Research indicates that peer relationships are among the most important to the second language acquisition process (Lightbown & Spada, 2006). At my school, we were encouraged to use all kinds of manipulatives, allowed the space and the freedom to make errors, and praised for being creative and collaborative. This preschool, and many others, offered an almost ideal environment for second language acquisition. What we must do as teachers of English Language Learners at every grade and age level is to attempt to create as ideal an environment as possible for their language acquisition to blossom. That takes critical and creative thinking on the part of teachers, and guarantees the opportunity for critical and creative thinking among learners.

Chapter 2
Language Acquisition

Second language acquisition (SLA) research has given us a growing understanding of optimum conditions, environments and strategies for language acquisition. This chapter will explore key ideas from that research as well as introduce the Habits of Mind and how these two areas can be joined to create good practice in teaching speakers of other languages. An understanding of how language is acquired and how critical and creative thinking is stimulated can help teachers to develop creative language learning activities of their own and to recognize good activities in books and from other sources. The best activities help learners to acquire language while engaging their problem-solving abilities, communication, collaboration and higher-order thinking skills. By housing activities within a framework of the Habits of Mind, we can develop thought and language simultaneously, thus turning theory into practice.

The Habits of Mind (HoM) align very closely with best practices in second language acquisition methods, activities and techniques. This is because language and thought are so closely interrelated that it is virtually impossible to separate them. All good language learning activities are necessarily also good thinking activities as we rely heavily on language to think abstractly. By couching language learning activities within the Habits of Mind, teachers are engaging students in an authentic use of language that is a necessary vehicle into academic discourse, as well as social interaction.

As a young teacher of language learners, I had the opportunity to work in a variety of challenging and interesting environments. In the six years after I finished my Masters in TESOL, I worked in California, Costa Rica, Morocco and Florida. My experiences in each location added to my knowledge of how language is acquired and contributed to my bag of tricks as a language teacher. I started out my career in bilingual kindergarten in Salinas, California. There I became adept at working with learners of limited economic means who had very few resources at home and who all came from the same language background. This situation ensured that I learn to utilize the resources I had available and make do with certain limitations. It also demanded that I come up with activities and ideas that were engaging, personal, meaningful and collaborative, as that was the only way to keep the attention of such young learners. All of these characteristics are essential to LAF activities.

Although I loved being a bilingual kindergarten teacher, I left after only one year to pursue a teaching career abroad. I accepted a position with a Central American Peace Scholarships (CAPS) program in Costa Rica. There, I was privileged to work with middle school, high school, and college students of low economic means who had been granted scholarships to study in the United States. These students had been accepted into three-month intensive English programs to learn as much English as they could and receive cross-cultural training before traveling to the United States. During the first summer in Costa Rica, I truly became a language teacher. The opportunity to work daily in an intensive program with the lowest level learners for a three-month period allowed me to practice every single teaching idea that I had ever heard of, and then some. I also discovered that I was able to create my own interesting language activities to a greater extent than many of my fellow teachers. I soon found that this was because I had such a strong theoretical foundation of knowledge on how language is acquired that I had obtained during my Master's program in TESOL at

Monterey Institute of International Studies (now Middlebury at Monterey). There, we had taken classes in psycholinguistics, second language acquisition, methods of teaching and many more. The program I attended heavily emphasized theory of first and second language acquisition, as well as sociolinguistics and research-based approaches to pedagogy. Based on what I determined to be important in creating good environments for language acquisition, I was able to create my own interactive activities and adapt other activities I found in the books and the materials we were provided.

Another very helpful aspect of working in Costa Rica is that I worked with English teachers and cross-cultural trainers who had been trained at the School for International Training (SIT) in Vermont. These teachers had a wealth of engaging activities on hand to share with all of us. Although they had more knowledge of existing activities than I did, I found that my teacher-training program provided me with more background to develop my own activities for language learners. Furthermore, in CAPs we were put in teaching teams so that we were in constant collaboration with one another and could learn from one another, share ideas and create together. This allowed us to think interdependently and to work together to come up with many things we probably would not have come up with on our own. We were using Habits of Mind (HoM) and LAF activity characteristics without even knowing it.

By the time I left Costa Rica for a teaching position in Morocco, I was already supervising teachers and sharing what I had learned even while I continued to learn from my students and from the other teachers I worked with. Many times, English teachers overseas are not trained in TESOL. They have little to no knowledge of English teaching and are hired based solely upon the fact that they are native speakers of English. Although some of these teachers are probably not very successful, others thrive through the challenge of teaching their own language, and soon realize that it takes more than speaking a language to be able to teach it effectively. They often research teaching methods and techniques on their own and experiment with new ideas. Many of these untrained teachers helped me to put into words the ideas and concepts that I had accumulated over time regarding best practices for language learners based on how language is acquired. In explaining things to them by communicating with clarity and precision, they helped me to further refine and polish my ideas. We were thinking interdependently, striving for accuracy and finding humor in our teaching situations. Again, we were using HoM to create LAF based activities for our learners while becoming better teachers in the process.

First Language Acquisition

To understand how second language is acquired, it is good to first explore how first language is acquired. We all know that virtually all babies will develop their first languages within about five years to become fluent speakers of their native languages. The only exceptions to this rule are those children who are born with serious neurological complications, deaf children who are not recognized as deaf, and those who are so neglected from birth that they do not receive the linguistic input and interaction required to acquire language. Luckily, these cases are very rare. The few that have existed have taught us quite a bit of the importance of those early years in terms of language acquisition as well as socialization.

The first thing we all notice about babies is that they are tiny, helpless, and generally adorable. This, although it may not seem so on the surface, is an important part of language acquisition. Babies need us for everything. They count on us for food, shelter, company, cleanliness and most importantly, love. They cannot survive without us. We, in turn, are captivated by their cuteness and strive to meet all their needs in any way we can. In short, we love them and they love us as caregivers. This mutual love and adoration creates a relationship and an environment that is ideal for language acquisition. It is warm and accepting, repetitive and comforting, personal and meaningful, collaborative and interactive, engaging and empathetic, contextual and kind.

Often one of the first things we do as adults when we discover that a baby is on the way is to talk to the baby in utero. This practice is common among individuals in many cultures and is a window into the importance of language in the process of building relationships and carrying our species forward. The mother will begin to have conversations with her tummy, talking about the future, declaring her love for the as-yet-unseen offspring, and musing aloud about how wonderful life will be when baby arrives. The father or other family members may offer their two cents, sometimes encouraging baby still in utero to become a fan of a certain sports team, or to look forward to the many things that they will do together after baby arrives. Parents begin to learn to be parents before a baby is even born, and talking to the baby in utero is a part of beginning to create that all-important relationship. Big brothers and sisters may also join in with their expressions of affection, and sometimes of jealousy and resentment. One friend of mine reported that her toddler yelled, "I hate you! You ruin everything!" to his unborn baby sister during a tantrum resulting from his mother not being able to slide down the slide with him due to her growing belly. Sibling rivalry can apparently begin at the fetal stage.

Some parents will sing and read to babies before birth. A whole industry of music to stimulate critical thinking in babies and to create mindful babies has developed to profit from parents' best intentions. Of course, not all cultures or all families within cultures do these things. The socio-economic group of the parents, their religious or non-religious beliefs, and the society they live in all influence the nature and the extent to which they communicate with babies before and shortly after birth, and no one way is necessarily superior to another. The essential fact is that parents and others will communicate with babies even before seeing them. We even have research evidence that babies both hear and listen in the womb, and what they hear and listen to affects their vowel formation after birth so they are already being tuned in to their native language. (Moon, Lagercrantz & Kuhl, 2013). Studies show that babies will recognize their mother's voices at birth, and many parents have noticed babies in utero startling at loud noises in the environment.

At the moment of birth babies make their first discourse moves and in many families, they begin to monopolize and control family interactions. They are powerful communicators. Their first move, if we are lucky, is a loud and lusty cry. As parents, we immediately respond to this sign of life and first baby-instigated communication with our own words, our smiles and our comforting arms. We continue to respond to cries throughout their babyhood, often recognizing that different tones and volumes in the crying melody can mean different things. A caregiver will often hear a baby cry and immediately declare what the problem is, identifying hunger, a wet diaper, fear, tiredness, illness, boredom or something else. More importantly, the caregiver responds with language and the meeting of baby's needs. Therefore, baby learns that a cry gets a response and continues to use this method of communication for quite a bit longer than most parents appreciate. It is a very successful technique.

At a couple of months of age, babies begin to add to their discourse strategies by cooing. We can explain cooing as those happy baby sounds that make many of us smile, melt, and pay lots of attention to baby. Who can resist an adorable cooing infant sucking a chubby fist and smiling? Babies soon discover that cooing works like a charm to generate positive attention from caregivers who often respond by cooing back and talking softly and sweetly to baby. They may also show baby toys, sing, or cuddle the cooing baby. This prolonged interaction stimulates baby's discourse practice by engaging baby in turn-taking events that mirror the question/answer sequences of true discourse. Adults and older children capture the attention of the baby with interesting sounds coming out of their mouths and the gestures and body language they use. Babies take in all the information and begin to accumulate a set of strategies and techniques to enhance their language acquisition process and to become full-fledged members of their native cultures.

Soon after the cooing stage, babies will progress to babbling. Adults and older children will respond, expand and most importantly give meaning to their babbles. We will turn the baby's ma-ma-ma babble in to the word Momma, or da-da-da to the word Dada, or ba-ba-ba to the word Baba and declare the baby has said her first word! Was the baby actually saying an actual word that she knows the meaning of? Probably not. She was just experimenting with sound, but she lives in a world where adults and older children will give meaning to her sounds, repeat them back to her endlessly, express joy and excitement when she strings a few babbles together and encourage her in every way to keep learning language. And she does. Notice how similar the words for immediate and important family members and significant baby things are across languages and cultures. The words mama, papa, baba, dada, tata, and more can be found in multiple languages and are often baby's first words.

But how do babies do it? How do these tiny, adorable, non-literate human beings discover how to understand and create language so efficiently? First language acquisition theories can be briefly summarized in the following way:

- **Behaviorism:** Babies are learning through habit formation and repetition of what they hear. This school of thought is associated with B.F Skinner (1957) and argues that reinforcement and imitation are the essential aspects of how language is acquired and the baby's linguistic environment is paramount.

- **Innatism:** Babies are biologically pre-programmed to acquire language. Their brains contain some universal principles of language similar to a template that allow them to figure it out when they are in language-rich environments. This school of thought is associated with Chomsky (1959), who pointed out in a response to Skinner that behaviorism can't explain how it is that babies end up understanding much more about language and how it works than what they were exposed to in their environment.

- **Interactionism:** Babies learn by interacting with caregivers in a natural way and in an environment that contextualizes language and includes modified input and scaffolding from those caregivers. This view, often associated with the work of Vygotsky (1978), emphasizes the importance of social interaction as part of language acquisition. Vygotsky posited that early childhood language development depends on a 'zone of proximal development' formed between a child and a more knowledgeable adult engaging in social interaction. In this zone the child is able to learn from the adult.

When we look at these three theories closely and pay attention to research in first language acquisition, a winning theory seems to emerge: interactionism. This is because interactionism is the most comprehensive of the theories. We have evidence that babies do much more than what behaviorism alone would suggest—that they learn language through repetition, imitation, reinforcement and habit formation. Of course many babies and toddlers do seem to repeat everything like little parrots, but, importantly, not all of them do. In my own family, I had both children who were repeaters and those who never repeated a thing, yet they all learned language. Behaviorism does not account for that variability, nor does it explain why children come up with 'novel utterances,' language they have never heard before. For example, my oldest daughter was very fond of the expression, "It's mines!" I can guarantee you that she never heard anyone say, "It's mines!" to her. She came up with that on her own. But how?

That is where innatism comes in, the idea that we are all born with a sort of universal set of language principles in our heads, allowing us to learn language and to express ourselves in language. These principles presumably include giving us the chance to create novel utterances such as, "it's mines." Clearly, the baby in this example is conveying a meaning and using grammar to do so, the only problem is that she is not using standard grammar. She is overgeneralizing the final -s that shows possession in the third person to the first person. She is taking an expression she has undoubtedly heard such as, "it's hers," or "it's Shihan's" and adding an -s to the word 'mine' to demonstrate possession when that is not necessary as the word already carries possession in its meaning. She is overgeneralizing a rule of language, demonstrating that she understands that language has rules, even though she could never put that idea into words at such a young age. She created a grammatically 'incorrect' sentence that is perfectly understandable.

On the flip side of this idea, Chomsky (1957) famously gave the example, "Colorless green ideas sleep furiously," to demonstrate how we can all create grammatically 'correct' sentences that are nonsensical. It also demonstrates how we can create sentences we have never heard before that can be understood by others: novel utterances. A sentence needs to contain both syntax that makes sense in the language, and semantic integrity in order to be meaningful. This sentence lacks the semantic integrity though the syntax works. Every single one of us who speaks a language can create a brand new sentence that we have never heard before but that can easily be understood by anyone who understands that language. You may have never heard the exact sentence that I am typing right here before in your entire life, and yet you are understanding it, aren't you? Or, for a more obvious example, I know you have never heard this: *Yesterday, while I was skipping along the brittle edge of a nonfat yogurt container, my thoughtful llama turned into a growling purple pumpkin.*

I am certain you have never heard that sentence before or seen it written, and yet right now you are picturing it in your mind. It is a ridiculous sentence full of words and ideas that don't normally occupy the same space, yet the understanding of the sentence is immediately within your reach. Innatism explains that we are able to do this amazing task of understanding language and producing novel utterances by the magic within our human brains that allows us to figure it out.

Innatist perspectives also help us to understand other developmental errors in addition to grammatically incorrect novel utterances and overgeneralized grammar markers. Babies will overextend word meanings. This can be seen when a baby first learns a word for an animal such as a dog and overgeneralizes the word 'dog' to any four legged animal they see, or 'daddy' to any man they encounter. My eldest daughter, whose father is Moroccan and darker skinned that the rest of our family, used to shout out 'lebes' to any dark skinned man she saw, regardless of their nationality. She clearly associated the word 'lebes' (or 'labas,' Moroccan Arabic for 'how are you?') with her father, and her father with all darker skinned men. Once she learned more about language and realized that only her father understood that word, she stopped doing that.

Our language learning brains truly are amazing, but innatist theory cannot fully explain how we acquire language as babies. What we have inside simply is not enough—we need to be interacted with over time in a language-rich environment in order to acquire language. We know from tragic cases that a child who has not been raised in an interactive, language-rich environment will never fully acquire language, and that there is a critical period during which this needs to happen. The Critical Period Hypothesis (CPH) posits that children who are not given access to language within an interactive, language-rich environment in early childhood will never fully acquire it (Lightbown & Spada, 2011).

In order to acquire language we need a supportive environment chock-full of interaction, and the kind of interaction that is given to babies is usually the ideal. We, as adults and older children, naturally, and without one single class in linguistics, provide an ideal language acquisition environment for babies by responding to them in ways that are personal, meaningful, repetitive, interactive, culturally relevant, engaging, empathetic, playful, loving, and promote higher order thinking. We tend to use child-directed speech with babies (Snow, 1995), also known as 'modified input' that includes talking about the here and now, using a higher pitch, simplifying our sentences, stressing key words and plenty of repetition. But how do we do it? By simply responding to babies needs and providing them with natural, and contextualized language at every turn. The table below shows how.

Age/ Stage	What are babies doing?	How are adults and older children responding?	What does it mean in terms of language acquisition?
In the womb	At first **hearing,** then **listening,** and occasionally responding to sound with movement	**Talking** to belly, using hand pressure/body language to communicate, providing music and, in some cases, reading	We are already giving babies the rhythm and the sounds of our language before they are born. We are already considering them part of our culture.
At birth, through the toddler years, and sometimes longer	**Crying**	**Responding, comforting,** holding and meeting the needs of the baby. Sometimes singing, **asking questions, making statements and attributing meaning to the babies' cries.**	Our responses to babies' cries almost always include language, for example: "there, there…" "Are you hungry?" "Do you need a diaper change?" "You're just sleepy, aren't you?"
At a few months of age and for a few months	**Cooing** – those adorable baby sounds	Responding by smiling, mimicking the coos, encouraging more cooing, talking, playing, **interacting** in loving ways with the baby	We are letting babies know that they will get attention when they make noises other than crying, and that the attention they get is positive and interactive.
At around 6 months of age and for many months	**Babbling** – those repeated syllables such as "ba-ba-ba"	Responding by smiling, mimicking the babble, encouraging more babbling, talking, playing, and most importantly **attributing meaning** to the babble – declaring that the baby has created a word! Examples: Baby: da..da..da.. Father: Dada? Did you say Dada? Dada, Dada, here's Dada! Baby: da-da- Father: He said Dada! He said his first word, it's Dada! Dada is here, here I am. Dada Baby: Dada!	We are letting babies know that a particular sound combination such as ma-ma is just the ticket to more time with us, more attention, more understanding, excited and happy caregivers and ultimately baby getting what he wants: Mama.

Anywhere from around 12 months to 24 months. By the age of 2 many (but not all!) children produce about 50 words	**First words and word chunks** such as, "bye-bye" or very short sentences, sometimes referred to as 'telegraphic sentences' such as: "Baby go bye-bye."	Responding by smiling, repeating the words, encouraging more words and repetition, talking, playing, confirming meaning and **extending the interaction,** adding to the first words. Examples: Baby: No baf! Mom: No bath? You don't want a bath? Baby: No baf! Mom: But you love your bath! Look here's your rubber ducky! Let's play with the water toys… Baby: Ducky! Mom: Yes, your rubber ducky, look how happy he is your in the bath! Yay, Let's sing the bathtime song….	We are letting babies know that language is an important part of how we relate to them and that they are powerful discourse partners. They can control conversations and lead us to topics of interest to them, and the more they talk to us the more attention we pay to them and the more they get what they want.
Age 2 and over all the way to around age 5	**Longer and more complex words and sentences**	Responding by encouraging more words, repetition, talking, playing, confirming meaning, **extending and adding to the interaction,** asking follow up questions for clarification and thinking, providing more and different kinds of input such as songs, videos, books and movies, and generally providing a socially interactive and appropriate space for children to acquire language.	We are letting babies know that there is a lot to learn by using language and that it opens up a world of possible activities that we can share together. We are also encouraging them to think critically and creatively through play, questioning and providing them with language rich resources such as books and videos.

There is an enormous amount of research and data available on first language acquisition (FLA) for those who are interested (see Berko-Gleason & Bernstein-Ratner, eds., 2009). For our purposes, as teachers of language learners, we want to know what the key aspects of first language acquisition are that can be used to inform our teaching practice. We want to borrow what we can from the highly effective FLA process and implement that as much as we can in second language classrooms. So, what are these key ideas?

Key Points about FLA that we should know for SLA

- Infants do not learn language through overt teaching; they learn in a natural, socially interactive environment.
- Children learn language by figuring out a set of language rules. We have evidence of this through novel utterances and developmental language errors made by babies such as overgeneralization and overextension errors.
- Children have to figure out the phonology, morphology, syntax, semantics, and discourse of a language in order to become fluent speakers, and they do it all simultaneously.
- It takes years of interacting in a language-rich environment to fully acquire a langauge.
- A child learns language with the help of modified input or 'caretaker speech.' This is the kind of speech that mothers and other caretakers use when they interact with their babies. It includes simplifying utterances, shortening them, repetition, and contextualizing language.
- The caregiver *scaffolds* the baby's utterances and provides the baby with new words and sentence structure.
  > Baby: Cookie.
  > Mother: You want a cookie?
  > Baby: Want cookie.
- Children acquire language in contextualized environments surrounded by people who love them, accept them as they are and are eager to hear to from them.
- Mistakes are accepted as a natural part of the process of language acquisition, and are even often considered cute and not corrected except through modeling.

Second Language Acquisition

Why talk so much about babies when we are presumably here to learn about how second languages are acquired? What we really want to know is how to best meet the needs of our second language learners while promoting their critical and creative thinking skills. The reason I like to talk first about babies is because their highly successful journey can teach us a lot about what to do in the classroom, as well as what *not* to do as teachers of language learners. Second languages are acquired in much the same way as first languages. Much of what we naturally do with babies is part of a language acquisition friendly (LAF) classroom. Yet, there are some significant differences between first and second language acquisition that we need to keep in mind. We can explore these by examining the similarities and differences between first and second language acquisition starting with theories that mirror those of first language acquisition.

Behaviorism: According to a behaviorist viewpoint, language acquisition relies heavily on habit formation, repetition and imitation (Lado, 1968). Many of us can recognize this perspective from experiences in language classrooms where much time was spent on drill and repeat activities such as those performed using the audio-lingual method where students repeat chorally and fill in blanks posed by the teacher with vocabulary in the target language. For example,

> T: This is a desk. Repeat.
> Class: This is a desk.
> T: This is a pen.
> Class: This is a pen.
> T: This is a _____ (points to desk)
> Class: This is a desk.
> Etc.

Innatism: According to this perspective, second language learners were once babies biologically pre-programmed to acquire language, and their brains still contain a kind of mechanism that allows them to figure out and acquire more languages. This point of view is emphasized by researchers who point out that second language learners eventually know more language forms than what they could have learned in the classroom, and commit developmental language errors similar to babies regardless of their first languages (White, 2003; Cook, 2003). For example, overextending the meaning of words such as using the word 'car' to mean any vehicle, overgeneralizing the past tense -ed marker where it does not belong ("I singed a song") and producing novel utterances they have never heard such as, "Good eat!" (to mean bon appetit).

Interactionism: Second language acquisition researchers have built on Vygotsky's ideas about a zone of proximal development for first language learners in which social interaction promotes language acquisition. These researchers also borrow heavily from Krashen's monitor model hypothesis (Krashen, 1982). The monitor model is such an important part of how thinking about language teaching has evolved in the past half century that it demands a deeper look.

Krashen proposed that in order to acquire language, the following conditions should be met:

- There should be a low **affective filter** present during learning activities so that language input can be received. The affective filter is like an invisible wall between the learner and what is being taught. In order to maintain a low affective filter in the classroom, learners should be comfortable and relaxed.
- Learners should receive **comprehensible input**, or i+1, so that they can understand what is being said without being overwhelmed with too much new linguistic information. Teachers need to modify input by different means, such as by using body language, visuals, repetition, rephrasing and other strategies so that learners can understand what they are trying to teach them.

- Learners should be encouraged to turn off their **monitor** or internal correction device. Learners who have their internal monitor on all the time due to worry about making mistakes will not be able to acquire language as well as those who keep it off. Teachers should allow for errors in the classroom as part of the natural process of language acquisition.

- Teachers need to understand that there is a **natural order** of language acquisition that indicates that certain grammar rules will be learned in a predictable way. Such as in first language acquisition, certain forms are learned before others and it is a poor use of time to teach things that are learned later in the 'natural order' since these will probably not be acquired until earlier forms are acquired.

- It is preferred that a language be **acquired** naturally (as in FLA) rather than **learned** traditionally. Traditional learning implies memorization of rules and overt correction of errors. Acquisition implies more opportunities to receive input in a natural way.

Krashen (1982) asserted that second language learners need only be exposed to comprehensible input in low-stress situations, without too much worry about mistakes, in order to acquire language. Since its proposal, this five-part hypothesis has come into question because it is virtually impossible to prove empirically and neglects to take into account the role of interaction. However, it continues to be fundamentally important to how communicative classrooms are structured.

Second language researchers built on Krashen's model, agreeing that comprehensible input is essential but ascertaining that learners also need prolonged social interaction in order to acquire language. This interaction includes modified input from interlocutors, comprehension checks, repetition, paraphrasing and negotiation of meaning with the learner (Long, 1993 & 1996; Pica, 1994; Gass, 1997). In interactional contexts, informational exchange occurs in varied and numerous ways. According to Long (1993) and other researchers, comprehensible input both fosters acquisition and encourages the output that is essential for fluency to develop. Therefore, activities for language learners should not only be comprehensible, but also interactive and include negotiation of meaning (Ellis, 1991).

In further research stemming from interactionist theories, some researchers have suggested that learners also need to produce language in order to acquire it, known as the comprehensible output hypothesis (Swain, 1985). Yet another aspect of language learner acquisition that researchers have suggested is that nothing is learned unless a learner becomes explicitly aware or 'notices' it (Gass, 1983 and Schmidt, 1990, 2001). Swain (2001) suggests that language learning demands both cognitive and social interactive elements. According to this perspective, learners must pay attention to both form and meaning in order to acquire language while engaged in interactions. Lantolf (2001) and others suggest sociocultural perspectives that view language acquisition as a socially mediated activity that eventually becomes internalized with social interaction providing language learners with the raw material they need (Dörhyei, 2009 and Swain, 2010).

Tied to interactionist-based theories is the role of feedback given to language learners. If social interaction is necessary and a negotiation of meaning between learner and language expert is fundamental, then a closer look at the nature of that interaction is required. Researchers have found that during this negotiation, error correction often takes place in both natural and classroom settings. In a traditional language classroom, errors are often corrected on the spot and with overt measures. However, in natural interactions it is more common to find errors either ignored when they do not interfere with meaning (such as pronunciation errors where the learner is understood) or corrected through recasting of learner language or modeling of the correct form (Lyster & Ranta, 1997). Teachers who implement recasting and modeling of corrected errors, offer wait time to give learners extra time to formulate responses, and provide scaffolds for language learners to support interactions and understanding are utilizing techniques that do not interrupt interaction. In this way teachers are creating an environment where interaction can flow more naturally and lead to further negotiation of meaning and language practice. Giving learners feedback in response to the output they are producing is an essential part of a classroom environment built around a theory of social interaction. Modification makes input comprehensible for L2 learners in much the same way that caretaker speech makes input comprehensible for babies.

Pica (1987) transforms our understanding of interactions by introducing the idea of social status. Social status differences give rise to disparity in conversations, for example, lower status people may not be allowed to ask questions, or may be discouraged from making suggestions (child vs. adult, employee vs. boss). For learners in classrooms to experience the second language as it is used in the real world, a variety of interactions, including different interlocutors interacting for varied purposes, is necessary.

Ellis (1991), in a critical review of the literature surrounding interactionism as a second language acquisition hypothesis, proposed the following:

- While comprehensible input facilitates second language acquisition, it is neither necessary nor sufficient for acquisition to take place.

- Interaction that includes negotiation of meaning and features modified input for learners make acquisition possible. These modifications need to provide learners with input they comprehend, the chance to notice new features of language, and compare the new features to their own output.

- When interaction requires that language learners modify their initial output, the process of integration is facilitated.

While there is still much research to be done on second language acquisition, and not all researchers agree on how much interaction, error correction, modified input, or attention to form is necessary, it is generally agreed that interaction in the second language classroom that includes comprehensible input and engaged output is necessary and valuable. This idea, and how to achieve it, is the basis for the activities that are offered in this book and housed under the term Language Acquisition Friendly (LAF) activities.

Key Points about SLA that teachers should know:

- Most second language learners are not able to acquire language in a natural environment in the same way as first language learners. Many are taught in classrooms or in a combination of classroom and new cultural context.
- Second language learners, much like first language learners, learn a set of language rules, either by figuring them out, or by being explicitly taught rules. We see evidence of second language learners figuring out rules when they overgeneralize certain rules such as adding an -ed regular past ending in English or plural -s to places these don't belong. They may also overextend word meanings and produce novel utterances they have never heard.
- Second language learners have to figure out the phonology, morphology, syntax, semantics, and discourse of a language in order to become fluent speakers. In a natural language acquisition setting, these subsystems of language are not focused on separately.
- It takes years of interacting in a language-rich environment to fully acquire a language. This is the same for both first and second language learners.
- A second language learner learns with the help of modified input, sometimes called 'foreigner talk.' This is the kind of speech that teachers and others use when they interact with learners in order to create comprehensible input. This type of speech includes simplifying utterances, shortening them, body language, repetition, and contextualizing language—just like caretakers do for first language learners but with different topics and no need for a high-pitched voice.
- Language teachers often *scaffold* and extend learner utterances and provide learners with new forms of language:
    > LL: I happy.
    > T: You are happy? Great! I am happy too. Why are you happy today?
    > LL: I am happy because I get an A.
    > T: You are happy because you got an A? Good job!
- Just like first language acquirers, second language learners need contextualized environments surrounded by people who encourage and support them, accept them as they are, interact with them in personal and meaningful ways, and provide a low-stress and welcoming atmosphere.

We can learn a lot from babies. They are persistent, they think flexibly, they are creative, they respond with wonderment and awe, and they naturally apply many of the other HoM to their language acquisition process. Although first and second language acquisition is not exactly the same, and we cannot treat our second language learners in the exact same way we treat babies, we can provide for them many of the linguistic and contextual environments that babies enjoy. We can encourage our language learners to utilize many of the strategies that babies utilize naturally in their language acquisition process, including the Habits of Mind.

Chapter 3
What being Language Acquisition Friendly (LAF) is all about

I started my teaching career thinking that I knew just about everything I needed to know about how to create and deliver good language lessons to learners. After a short time teaching, I realized I still had a lot to learn. Though my graduate program had prepared me with all of the theory and much of the practice that I needed as a novice teacher, when I put my knowledge into practice, my methods, activities and strategies did not always work. Sometimes I was hindered by textbooks and workbooks that did not seem to be helpful, but that needed to be used in order to meet the expectations of administrators. While spending time using the books in class, I often lost the attention of my students. Other times, when I chose to ignore the books, even my best planned activities flopped for no reason that I could determine. Certain students wanted to stick to the book and did not see value in the interactive and engaging (according to me) activities I had developed. They wanted more of a focus on form when I was going for more of a focus on meaning. These students were worried that if they were having 'fun' then they were wasting valuable class time during which they should be learning language rules and drilling pronunciation. It sometimes felt as though my class was simply not in tune with my teaching, or that a small group of learners that was uncooperative had the ability to sour the entire class. At these times my students became unwilling to engage in the activities I had prepared despite my best efforts.

Each of my many failures as a teacher taught me something new. One thing I learned early on is that it was not an option to give up. I had to go into my classrooms every day and try again to capture the attention of my learners while giving them as much valuable information and practice with the target language as possible. Being a new teacher was an exercise in practicing the Habits of Mind. I had to think flexibly when what I was doing was not working, I had to persist when I wasn't getting through to my learners, I had to find humor when situations felt disastrous, and I had to listen with empathy and understanding to my learners when they disagreed with my approach.

After several years, a variety of experiences, and much thoughtful reflection, I started to understand that some of my activities were lacking certain elements that were essential to making an activity work. Other activities had all of the necessary elements but I was simply not explaining them well enough. I was not giving clear enough directions. I had to strive for accuracy and communicate with clarity and precision so that my learners could understand what I was asking them to do and why. I had to convince them that an interactive and communicative language classroom was their best chance for language acquisition, and I had to convince myself that their opinions mattered as much as mine even if they had no training in TESOL. If my learners did not buy into the way I was teaching my class, then all of my efforts would be useless. They had to understand and appreciate the strategies I was trying to use with them in order for those strategies to succeed.

Once I began training teachers, I realized that I had to write down and really flesh out the ideas I had developed after years of teaching language learners. I developed a list of characteristics that I felt were necessary in order for learners to truly benefit from a language classroom. I went about adding to this list over time and changing it, realizing that I had left some important things off the list. Along the way, my most valuable teachers were the learners themselves. They showed me what worked and what didn't, what needed more explanation and what was clear. They made me a better language teacher and a reflective practitioner.

I used to call these characteristics of good language lessons that I developed over time, 'ESOLish.' I meant that they were good for ESOL students, English Language Leaners (ELLs), but in reality they are good for anyone learning any second language, and the word ESOLish did not accurately capture that concept. I decided to rename my list Language Acquisition Friendly and call it LAF-ish, or LAF for short. I hope that this is a better name for this list and that this list is a valuable tool for teachers who are striving to create and implement activities that will promote success in the language acquisition process of their learners.

The following are the characteristics that I have determined belong in every good activity for language learners in the classroom: the LAF list. I strive to prepare lessons that contain all (or most) of these characteristics. The activities you will find in this book have been created with these characteristics in mind, and you will find a LAF aspects list for each activity. You may find that you have more characteristics to add to the LAF list for your particular class or your teaching style. Feel free to add to the list in any way that meets the needs of your situation, but try to conserve as much of what is here as possible for best results. Below the list, you will find a more detailed explanation of every element of the list and an explanation of why you should create activities that include that element.

The LAF List

- Be interactive
- Give clear directions in multiple ways, including modeling
- Use authentic language
- Encourage critical and creative thinking skills
- Make activities personal and meaningful
- Employ cooperative learning structures
- Value multiple perspectives
- Design engaging and motivating activities
- Design activities that are purposeful
- Enhance activities with graphic organizers and visuals
- Utilize body language for clarity and comprehension
- Allow for natural repetition within activities
- Build on prior knowledge, including the L1
- Error correct with empathy and thoughtfulness

---

1. Be interactive

Interaction is always the right answer when we are looking at language acquisition. The more students are able to use the language, the more likely they are to learn and attain fluency in the language. This is best achieved in the classroom by promoting active learning through information gap, task-based and other structures that promote interaction, cutting down on overt correction during the time of an activity, and increasing cooperative learning tasks. The interactionist theory states that "students acquire an L2 with greater ease, and at a quicker rate if they are able to constantly interact with peers who speak the target language with greater proficiency" (Ellis, 1991). In a language classroom where everyone is a second language learner, groupings can be established that mix weaker learners with stronger learners, and teachers also act as interaction partners. Through continuous interactions with negotiation of meaning, language learners receive comprehensible input and begin to produce output, thus encouraging language acquisition.

2. Give clear directions

No matter how wonderful your activity is, if your students don't understand what want them to do, it will flop. It is extremely important that you give your language learners clear directions that they are able to follow and that you do this in multiple ways. The lower the language level, the more ways you need to give directions for any activity that is new and might be confusing. It is a good idea to give both oral and written directions, examples and modeling whenever possible. When learners understand teacher expectations they are more likely to follow directions and take risks using the target language. Making activities clear increases comprehensible input and helps to lower the affective filter that learners might be feeling in the classroom.

3. Use Authentic Language

Authentic language is the language that native speakers use when they are engaged in oral and written discourse. It is the 'real' way that they speak and write rather than what is often found in textbook dialogues for second language learners. This is especially important for teens and young adults because of their need to sound like others their own age so that they can engage in meaningful conversations with their peers. The idea is to use authentic language as much as possible with students and show them that the way people speak in everyday conversation is not necessarily the way that talk is portrayed in many textbooks. Using small clips from movies and interviews can help in this area. Below is a segment from a dialogue in a book compared with a transcript of two teenage English speakers.

Each conversation is about the same idea—going to a party on Saturday night—yet the conversations are very different. I use this and other examples to show my students that there are many ways to say the same thing, and that they need to be attune to how native speakers actually use language so that they will be able to understand them better and thus interact with them more effectively. We look at the ages of the people involved, the situation and other variables. I tell my students that I will try to use authentic language with them during oral language activities as much as possible in order to prepare them for using language in the real world.

By examining the authentic language used by native speakers and utilizing what we learn in the classroom, we are also practicing the habits of Listening with Understanding and Empathy, Thinking Flexibly, and Communicating with Clarity and Precision.

> ESL handout:
> A: Would you like accompany me to a party on Saturday night?
> B: Yes, I would love to.
> A: Wonderful, I'll pick you up at seven.

Native speaker transcript:
A: Want to go to that getty on Saturday?
B: I'm down.
A: Cool.

4. Encourage Critical and Creative Thinking Skills

The use of higher-order thinking skills is imperative in teaching language. If students are not given access to the vocabulary and the grammar that is involved in thinking on a complex level, they cannot verbally engage in complex learning activities. In order to assist a learner's understanding of academic text and tasks, she must be exposed to these texts and tasks while concurrently being given rich contextual support. By integrating the HoM into language learning activities, there is a guarantee that critical and creative thinking will be part of every activity practiced. I always try to make sure that even if much of my activity revolves around one of the lower levels of Bloom's pyramid, I am also using questioning strategies and tasks that are best represented by one of the highest levels of the pyramid. Keeping the HoM in mind makes this easy.

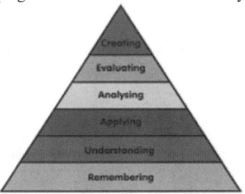

5. Make activities personal and meaningful

When students of all ages find that the lessons they encounter have personal relevance and are meaningful to them, they are able to retain more, are more engaged, and enjoy learning more. This can be done with any lesson if the teacher uses a little bit of imagination. Teachers can help learners make connections between their lives and what they're learning. In order to do this well, it is a good idea to get to know your learners, their likes and dislikes, their challenges and their passions. It is a good idea to get to know something about their home cultures and languages. Learners are the experts that can teach this to you. It is also a good idea to share cultural and linguistic information about yourself. In this way you are creating a connection between yourself and your students that will make teaching them easier and more rewarding for you. Trying to make connections between a language lesson and a learner's life encourages that learner, validates that learner and provides a culturally relevant classroom environment.

6. Employ cooperative learning structures

Research on the use of cooperative learning structures has demonstrated their effectiveness for language learning. It is important to create heterogeneous cooperative groups that feature face-to-face interaction, positive interdependence, and a do-able task. When learners are put in groups and told to 'discuss' a topic but not given specific roles and information creating a positive interdependence between them, discussion may not take place. Stronger learners may dominate the discussion or students may decide they don't need to discuss at all. By giving individual learners a different piece of the puzzle in order

30

to complete an activity, the need to interact cooperatively with one another is created. This need is met through the use of language. Cooperative learning goes beyond interaction for the sake of language practice; it creates the need to interact in order to complete a given task. In this way the focus becomes finishing the task rather than practicing language simply for the sake of practice, which is what some activities can look like. Be careful when preparing cooperative learning activities that one learner cannot complete the entire task by him or herself. Each learner must have a role that is integral to task completion and that cannot be usurped by another learner. These roles cannot merely be to give an opinion, they must go beyond that to provide essential information.

7. Value diverse perspectives
In the past, I have called this aspect of LAF being 'multicultural.' However, many interpret this as the idea that we must always be teaching about other cultures and including information about other cultures in each lesson. That is not the idea. The idea is to allow, validate and recognize a variety of perspectives in each lesson. No matter where a language learner is from, their native language or cultural background, it is essential to recognize that they bring an important perspective to every class activity. By making activities that allow for more than one right answer or 'way of knowing,' learners are being validated. This is a step toward culturally relevant pedagogy and should always be employed in a language classroom. The idea must be clear that the classroom is a place to learn the target language but also a place that values the native language and culture and recognizes that it can support and contribute to the learning of the target language.

8. Design engaging and motivating activities
There is no reason that the language classroom can't be one of the most interesting and fun classes for learners. Language is part of virtually everything we teach and learn and any number of topics may be employed that encourage students to want to interact in the target language. Games, role plays and simulations are all designed to make language acquisition interactive and engaging and should be employed often in the language classroom. When learners are engaged in an activity, they are more likely to have low affective filters, thus lower stress and more openness toward learning. This makes language input more easily accessible. In addition, when learners are engaged in an activity they are more motivated to learn and to continue practicing the language. Finally, engaged learners are less focused on the language itself and more focused on whatever activity they are doing that is being done through the language. This mirrors how children learn their first languages; they are learning about the world as they learn language, not focused on the language itself. Similarly, second language learners who are learning through the language, while engaged in an activity that captures their interest, are able to practice and add to their language in a contextualized and interactive manner.

9. Design activities that are purposeful
When learners come across an activity that has a clear purpose and end goal, they are more motivated to complete that activity. If the purpose of the activity is simply to practice the target language, then that activity runs the risk of becoming a chore. In addition, stronger language learners will often dominate such an activity. When a language learning activity is housed within a purposeful or task-based activity, then learners are using language to complete the activity and find the 'solution' or accomplish the task. This takes a focus off of language while assuring that language is being used in more natural ways. These types of activities include information gap activities and task-based activities.

10. Enhance activities with graphic organizers and visuals

All learners can benefit from seeing a visual or a graphic organizer to help clarify the meaning of text or oral language. Those who are second language learners may especially need the additional context that a visual can provide in order to access meaning. Teachers have a multitude of possibilities at their disposal with the Internet, the actual environment, and by having students create their own visuals. With the wide availability of cell phones, a visual can be pulled up right away to help clarify a concept. In addition, a visual often engages a learner's attention in a way that language alone might not.

11. Utilize gestures and body language for clarity and comprehension

Much like a visual can help to clarify the meaning of language for a learner, the use of body language can provide context and clarity. Every culture in the world uses body language as part of the communication system. However, the meanings of gestures vary across cultures, as does the extent to which body language is used. An exploration of how body language is used across cultures within the language classroom can be an interesting and insightful discussion with learners who are culturally diverse. Many misunderstandings and miscommunications may be linked to misunderstood gestures. It is estimated by some experts that up to eighty percent of how we communicate is tied to body language. Teachers can utilize hand movements, facial gestures and other sorts of body language to make their lessons more comprehensible for learners. This is also important in modeling for learners how to make themselves understood by going beyond vocabulary they might already know. By giving learners multiple ways to express themselves, we are helping them to become communicatively competent.

12. Allow for natural repetition within activities

Repetition is an important part of language acquisition and it doesn't have to be boring. We repeat constantly during natural discourse, and when this type of repetition is incorporated within activities students get to hear things many times, reinforcing their understanding. Repetition does not mean drill and repeat. Doing this can lead to boredom and disengagement from learning. Natural repetition includes rephrasing what we are saying, comprehension checks that allow learners to hear a standard model and repeat, as well as activities that are designed so that repetition occurs as part of the activity.

13. Build on prior knowledge including the first language (L1)

The first language is a valuable resource in the second language classroom. Students use their understanding of first language phonology, syntax, morphology, discourse and semantics to relate to their new language. Cognates, borrowed words, and literacy knowledge from the L1 are all helpful in developing an understanding of the L2. Even transfer errors are useful in pointing out the differences between the two systems. In addition, in classrooms where learners share the same first language, discussion in the first language during activities to clarify concepts or to expand on understanding may be valuable. However, it is important to remember that doing an activity in the first language and then simply translating to the target language will deny learners valuable language practice in the language being learned.

14. Error correct with empathy and thoughtfulness

When individuals learning a second language are corrected for every error, the classroom tends to become quieter. Learners need a chance to figure out language, make errors (just like kids in the process of first language acquisition) and be able to negotiate for meaning by using a variety of discourse structures. When too much overt error correction is employed, learners are less likely to contribute and there is little chance for discovery learning. However, learners may not realize this. They will often ask teachers to correct them every time they make an error. I always explain to my learners why this is not necessarily a good idea. By overtly correcting errors every time language learners make them, a disruption of interaction will occur. By overtly pointing out mistakes to learners, many of them will feel intimidated and even hopeless and be less likely to speak and interact in the target language. They will turn on their internal correction monitors so high that they will refrain from using the language unless they are sure they are correct. This is never a good idea. Error correction is necessary, but it does not have to be overt or humiliating. We can correct errors through modeling the correct form when appropriate, or by selecting a time at the end of a lesson when we review errors as a whole class that came up during the lesson without the need to single out a specific learner. When a learner asks to be corrected, or asks whether they have said something correctly, it is okay to correct in that moment because they initiated the correction. However, it is wise to refrain from correcting most errors during an interaction unless they occlude meaning, and even then it is best done through asking for clarification from a learner and giving that learner an opportunity to self-correct.

15. Make sure that your lesson is adaptable

A good language activity is adaptable to different levels of learners. This ensures that language learners can receive comprehensible input. Teachers often know how to regulate their language to be comprehensible, but sometimes an activity seems to demand too much of our learners. When this is the case, the activity must be adapted. This often means adding visuals, giving extra modeling, or simplifying the language demands. Other times, an activity is too easy for our more advanced learners. To adapt it to be more challenging, teachers can cut down on the time allowed for completion, take away visuals and/or include multiple steps that build on one another. By adapting activities, you will meet the needs of all of your language learners.

Chapter 4

What are the Habits of Mind and what do they have to do with Language Learning?

Why is it so easy to develop a bad habit, and so difficult to develop a good one? If good habits were as easily attained as bad ones, we would all be thoughtful and kind, composed and positive, and physically and mentally fit all of the time. Unfortunately, working out a few times, occasionally reflecting carefully on a tricky problem, or practicing random acts of kindness once in a while do not automatically lead to a lifetime of fitness, thoughtfulness or kindness. In fact, developing good habits is hard work with no end in sight. Good habits have to be consciously and continually worked on in order to become somewhat automatic. The trick is to love the work, but how can we do that? I believe that by learning about and incorporating Habits of Mind as teachers and learners, we can instill a culture of thoughtfulness, critical thinking, and creativity in the classroom. We can teach our students the habits that will help them to attain academic and career success while we learn along with them and strengthen our teacher/student relationships. Integrating the Habits of Mind in our learning activities can be one way for many of us to love the hard work of developing the positive and helpful thinking habits we need throughout our lives.

Fostering critical and creative thinking habits in the language classroom opens up a world of possibilities for teachers and learners. As teachers, we want to make sure that our language learners are prepared to encounter everything that will come their way linguistically so that they can negotiate a new language and culture successfully. Yet, our learners are all different and they will not all respond equally well to even the most well-prepared lessons. They come to us with different personalities, capabilities, wants and needs, and will end up pursuing different careers and exploring different experiences that call for different kinds of language. Therefore, we need to prepare them not only for the language usage we think they need and we reward in school, but for being able to negotiate language in all kinds of settings and under all kinds of circumstances.

What works for one learner will not work for all learners. Both teachers and learners need to be prepared to quickly change course when the path we are on is not working. Teaching is, therefore, a critical and creative thinking endeavor. It is a problem-solving activity that we participate in every day that demands a disposition to think critically and creatively. I believe that by using the HoM as a foundation for language learning, we can develop and nurture this disposition in our learners and ourselves. But what are these habits, and how do they fit into everything we want to accomplish?

A 'Habit of Mind' is a disposition toward behaving in an intelligent and reflective way when faced with a problem, the answer to which is not immediately evident. In other words, these habits encourage us to be thoughtful rather than reactive, creative rather than rote. As thinking teachers, we are interested in providing a wealth of valuable learning experiences that will prepare our learners to become capable and skilled problem solvers, to become thinkers that can think in more than one language.

Research indicates that there are certain characteristics of effective thinkers and problem solvers that can be taught; these are the Habits of Mind (HoM) as described by Costa &

Kallick (2008). Although 16 of these thinking habits are identified, that does not mean that there are only 16. These HoM are actually umbrella terms that are helpful in categorizing the kinds of dispositions we need to be adept at problem solving and the behaviors we require in order to put our problem solving skills to work. You will find that you are already familiar with the Habits as they are described, even if you are not yet familiar with the specific terminology. You will probably also find that it is easier to read about them and talk about them than it is to put them into daily practice.

In order to become intelligent thinkers, we all have to learn the habits that promote intelligent thinking, and that means practicing those habits as often as possible at the times that they apply. We can incorporate training in the Habits of Mind into what we do every day as teachers without significantly modifying the curricular choices we make. The habits give us a set of lenses and skills to interact with content learning, as well as the practice we need in order to change course as needed. If the habits are practiced throughout the day's learning activities and beyond, they are much more likely to be put to use in situations where they are truly required. The following is a list of the 16 Habits of Mind with a short explanation of what each involves and how it can be connected to second language acquisition.

Habit of Mind	Explanation
Persistence	Staying focused and sticking to a task until it is done; reaching a goal and not giving up when a task becomes challenging. *Second language acquisition takes persistence.*
Managing Impulsivity	Thinking before reacting; staying calm thoughtful and deliberative. *Language learning requires patience.*
Listening with Understanding & Empathy	Stepping in to the shoes of another person by listening attentively and striving to understand where others are coming from. *Second language learners thrive in empathetic and understanding environments that include lots of listening.*
Thinking Flexibly	Finding more than one way to think about a problem; keeping an open mind to new ideas. *Language acquisition requires flexible thinking.*

Metacognition	Becoming aware of the way we think and react to others; what strategies we use while thinking and how others may think differently. *Language acquisition makes us aware of our own thinking.*
Striving for Accuracy	Wanting to accomplish good, careful work, checking our work and modifying as necessary until we do our best. *Language acquisition requires attention to accuracy.*
Applying Past Knowledge	Tapping into what we already know to build new knowledge on the foundation of our prior knowledge and experiences. *Language acquisition works with knowledge we have from our first languages.*
Questioning and Problem Posing	Keeping a questioning attitude; knowing what data are needed and developing questioning strategies to produce those data. Finding problems to solve. *Second language acquisition thrives in an environment of asking and answering questions.*
Thinking and Communicating with Clarity and Precision	Being clear and understandable in our communication; avoiding over-generalizations or ambiguity when clarity is necessary. *Language learners need extensive interactive practice in communicating with clarity in a new language.*
Gathering Data Through all the Senses	Tuning in to our surroundings by using all of our senses; becoming better observers by gathering information through taste, touch, sight, hearing and feeling the world around us. *Language learners need to learn to use contextual clues, including body language and surroundings, to clarify meaning when language is not comprehensible.*

Creating, Imagining, Innovating	Having the courage and the inspiration to try new things and to imagine new possibilities; using our creative talents to resolve problems and create interesting solutions. *Language acquisition is an inherently creative process where the learner must imagine a new sociolinguistic identity.*
Responding with Wonderment and Awe	Noticing the beauty and the wonder that surrounds us by taking the time to marvel at the incredible wonders that are available in nature and society. *Language learners are constantly learning new things about the target language and culture and can be encouraged to respond with wonderment at new cultural knowledge to add to their own.*
Taking Responsible Risks	Being willing to try new things and participate in new activities; having a sense of adventure and the courage to fail. *Making mistakes is a necessary part of language acquisition, and second language learners must take risks in the new language in order to learn.*
Finding Humor	Being able to laugh at oneself and at situations that are difficult or unexpected; using humor to manage the challenging aspects of our lives. *Language learners who are willing to laugh at themselves and their failed attempts in the new language are at a distinct advantage for prolonging and initiating interactions with native speakers.*
Thinking Interdependently	Fostering a sense of teamwork and the willingness and ability to accept the ideas and the perspectives of others. *Language learners can enhance their acquisition of the target language by interacting with others and working together on tasks interdependently.*

Remaining Open to Continuous Learning	Accepting that we are in a process of learning throughout our lives and that we will never know everything; being open to learning something new every day. *The process of acquiring a second language is a lifelong process. Language learners who are open to learning continuously feel less frustrated than those who wish to get it over with as quickly as possible.*

Adapted from: Costa, A. and Kallick, B. (2000) *Habits of Mind. A Developmental Series*. Alexandria, VA: Association for Supervision.

If we practice these habits on a regular basis, we are more likely to be able to employ them when needed and therefore make better, more thoughtful, and more rational decisions. The journey of learning that is possible through the Habits of Mind is a journey that we can take together with our language learners, as we all certainly have a lot to learn. We can begin by asking ourselves and our learners the following questions to get an idea of which Habits we need to work on the most, and which come more naturally to each of us. Try answering the following questions for yourself and give them to your language learners if they are at a level that they can understand them. You can also adapt these questions to make them easier to comprehend for lower-level language students by simplifying the linguistic demand and providing examples.

Answer YES, SOMETIMES or NO to each of the following:

1. Do I tend to give up on things too easily? Do I tend to quit activities that I might not be good at right away or avoid those activities altogether?
2. Do I really listen and try to understand when I don't agree with someone or when I'm busy? Do I tend to interrupt while others are talking?
3. Can I laugh at myself when I make a mistake? Can I find humor in a situation that is difficult or challenging?
4. Do I never overreact, react too quickly or jump to conclusions before I have all of the information I need? Do I tend to blow up sometimes?
5. Do I think of new ways to look at things, and can I change my mind when introduced to new evidence? Can I be flexible and open-minded, or am I set in my ways?
6. Am I aware of my own thinking process when making decisions? Do I know why I do what I do?
7. Do I check my work to make sure it is accurate and clear? Am I careful when I am working or do I rush through things just to get them done?
8. Do I always look for new information? Am I curious about new ideas, and do I try new things? Am I willing to change my routine?
9. Do I use what I know from my past knowledge and experiences when facing new situations? Do I think back to what has happened before when I am trying to understand what is happening now?
10. Do I use all of my senses to learn about and explore the world? Am I willing to discover new ways of interacting with the world around me?
11. Do I use words effectively? Am I always adding to my vocabulary? and trying to be clear? Do I like to use words that are new to me?
12. Am I curious and do I let myself have a sense of wonder about the world?
13. Am I adventurous and willing to take reasonable risks? Do I take risks that are dangerous or unnecessary?
14. Do I know that I need to keep learning throughout my life and that I can and should continue learning throughout my life? Do I understand that I will never know everything and that what works now might not work later?
15. Do I really listen to others and learn from them? Do I give others a chance to work with me or do I tend to shut others off?
16. Do I ask lots of questions of others and myself when I am unsure of what to do, and do I enjoy solving problems?

If you were thoughtful and reflective in answering these questions, you should see that the HoM are not something that can be learned overnight, nor are they something that we may ever fully master. Most of us need to work on all of the HoM, but some come more naturally or easily than others. In the upcoming chapters of this book, we will explore the HoM in more detail and I will invite you on my journey in using these Habits for teaching language learners and training teachers to teach language learners. Understanding and implementing the HoM is not a one-day deal, it is a lifetime of practice, reflection and experience, and I am still on that path along with my learners.

Each of the chapters in this book will focus on creating LAF activities that highlight two of the HoM, contain anecdotes about how they are encountered and practiced in teaching, and suggest ideas and activities for implementing them remotely or in the classroom with language learners. The activities are divided into language skill areas of focus, but all of them integrate all of the language skills, or can be modified to do so. In addition, you will find activities that are more appropriate for younger learners or older learners, but most can be adapted according to age, interest and maturity level. The activities as written are designed for high beginner to high intermediate language learners, however most can be adapted to any level with a few modifications. I will show you how to adapt activities by simplifying them or making them more challenging, as well as offering remote learning adaptations. It is important to remember that as the teacher you know your own students best, and you will be able to see what works in your particular teaching situation, and how to adapt activities further to meet the specific needs of your learners. You will be using the HoM while teaching the HoM, as you will need to think flexibly and communicate with clarity and precision so that you and your learners can grow in your thinking together.

Often the content of your language lessons will determine what particular Habit or combination of Habits makes the most sense to practice, and how it can be practiced. Make sure to keep an open mind when you are looking at the ideas presented in this book. Although they may not work in exactly the way they are written for your specific learners, you can certainly adapt most of them to meet the needs of any group of language learners. After all, you have chosen to teach! This courageous choice indicates that you embrace a thinking challenge every day and that you are committed to providing your language learners with the tools they need to be successful problem solvers who think critically, creatively and consistently. Remember to encourage your learners to share their own language and culture acquisition stories and listen carefully when they do. This practice of listening will give you the tools you need to modify and create activities for your particular learners and ensure the establishment of an environment of empathy in your classroom.

LAF with the Habits of Mind

Habits of Mind Jigsaw

Focus On	Speaking, listening and reading
Language Functions	Describing, explaining, asking and answering questions
Grammar/Vocabulary Practiced	Present tense, past tense, modals, conditionals Vocabulary associated with Habits of Mind
Grouping Strategy	Individual, pair, whole group
LAF Aspects	<ul><li>Personal and meaningful – learners are expressing their own ideas.</li><li>Cooperative – when done in pairs or when learners build on one another's ideas during interaction.</li><li>Engaging – learners are engaged in the story and listening in order to complete the task.</li><li>Purposeful – students end up putting a jigsaw together, adding a physical component to their activity.</li><li>Interactive – learners share their ideas and interact while being questioned by a teacher.</li><li>Values diversity – learners demonstrate different perspectives with their responses.</li><li>Higher-order thinking – with more than one right answer, learners must think abstractly and consider various possibilities in order to complete the activity. They can be creative and analytical in their responses.</li></ul>
Materials	Provided reading of the Habits of Mind cut in to connecting jigsaw shapes; pencils or markers; large poster; glue or tape.

STEPS

- Use the reading provided below to read about the HoM with your learners.
- Break up the reading into 'jigsaw puzzle pieces.'
- Give each learner or pair of learners one Habits to focus on.
- Depending on the ages and language level of your learners, you may want to rewrite the reading and simplify it for better understanding.
- Once each learner or pair has had a chance to read and think about the HoM provided, come together and take turns explaining each one to the whole group and giving examples of what each looks like.
- As each person describes his or her Habit of expertise, everyone else listens, asks questions and designs a symbol to represent what that Habit looks like in real life. The symbols can be added to the jigsaw piece as illustrations of the Habit by having learners cut them out and glue them on the part of the reading they belong to.
- At the end of the activity, the pieces are attached to a poster board for a collaborative visual display of the Habits of Mind that everyone can refer to throughout the year.

The Habits of Mind
- HoM are a way to think and behave when we encounter problems that have no easy solutions.
- People who are great problem solvers use these Habits of Mind.
- HoM are thoughtful behaviors that can be helpful to us while we are learning, relating to one another and trying to reach our goals.

Persistence – This habit promotes sticking to a task without giving up. If you are being persistent, you also have to be patient with yourself. It may be very difficult to reach your goal, but you can keep trying and learning from the mistakes or failures you have made along the way. Successful language learners are persistent. They ask for help when they need it and they keep trying even when it is hard.

Listening with Understanding and Empathy – When we listen with understanding and empathy we are putting ourselves in someone else's shoes. This habit encourages us to really listen carefully to what other people are saying and to try to understand their points of view. By listening carefully and quietly we can learn a lot about one another and why we behave the way we do. Successful language learners have to do a lot of listening. Listening with empathy includes understanding that people from different cultures vary in behavior and interaction and we should avoid judging them or trying to change them.

Managing Impulsivity – This habit helps us to be in control of our words and our behaviors. It means that we are able to reflect rather than react to things thoughtlessly. When we are managing our impulsivity we will not end up saying things we regret later or behaving in ways that are counter-productive. Successful language learners need to manage their impulsivity when frustrated with the new language.

Metacognition – Metacognition is thinking about our own thinking. We can question ourselves and reflect on why we think and feel the way we do. It means that we take the time to be thoughtful and to consider why we may be thinking and feeling certain ways, and we can share these thoughts with others so that they can better understand us. Successful language learners are also learning a new culture and sharing our thinking helps us to understand our own culture, the new culture, and each other.

Responding with Wonderment and Awe – This habit promotes an appreciation of our surroundings and the wonders that we encounter every day. It reminds us to find the beauty in things that we may be taking for granted. Successful language learners often look for new things in the new language and culture they are learning to enjoy.

Creating, Imagining and innovating – This habit encourages us to use creativity and our imaginations in problem solving. Each of us is like an inventor of our own lives and we can often come up with unique solutions to the obstacles we encounter if we think creatively. Successful language learners need to be creative and innovative as they navigate a new language and culture.

Striving for Accuracy – This habit helps us remember to be as accurate or precise as we can when we are communicating. We want to be sure that others can understand what we are doing, and that they can appreciate our work. Successful language learners always strive for accuracy so that they can be understood.

Thinking Flexibly – Remember that there is often more than one right way of doing things. There can be many paths to solving a problem and sometimes when one of our solutions don't work, we need to find another solution. In order to do this we have to be open to thinking flexibly. Successful language learners must be flexible thinkers when they don't know a word or understand something in the new language. They must find a different way to figure out meaning.

Thinking Interdependently – This habit promotes working with other people to come up with ideas and solutions to problems. By listening to and asking questions of others we can expand our own ways of understanding a problem and build new ideas and strategies together. This habit is about teamwork. Successful language learners interact with others as much as they can.

Gathering Data Through All the Senses – Using all of our senses to figure out new ways of understanding the world around us. We usually concentrate on our sight and our hearing to get information but sometimes using our sense of touch, smell or taste can help us to gain a new perspective on an old problem. Successful language learners try to figure out language from context, including watching for visual clues to what is being said.

Taking Responsible Risks – Be willing to take a risk. If we are willing to take a risk and try something new or do something that might be a little bit out of our comfort zones, we are giving ourselves a chance to grow. The key is to be responsible in our risk taking. We want to make sure that we are not putting ourselves in danger or doing something that is contrary to our goals. Successful language learners risk making errors in their new language, they don't wait until they are fluent speakers to use the language.

Finding Humor – This habit encourages us to be able to find the humor in our daily lives, even when those lives can be challenging. Sometimes we need to laugh at ourselves when we are learning something new and accept that nobody is perfect and that it is okay to mess up. Finding the funny in what could be a difficult or uncomfortable situation allows us to relax and try again. It also helps us connect to others. Successful language learners know that sometimes their language errors are funny and can laugh at themselves.

Communicating with Clarity and Precision – We should be clear and precise with our words and our actions. We want to make sure that others truly understand our meaning and that we are able to communicate our meaning with precision. By being careful and thoughtful in what we write and say, we can be more certain that our communications turn out the way we intend them to. Successful language learners use all of their linguistic and non-verbal strategies to be as clear as they can.

Questioning and Problem Posing – This habit opens up the world as a place where we can discover new things through engaging with our own thinking and the thinking of others. When we ask questions we are automatically learning new things and taking in new points of view. We also need to question ourselves, especially when what we are doing is not working out the way we intended. By posing problems to ourselves and others, we are exercising our thinking brain and allowing ourselves to become better problem solvers. Successful language learners ask a lot of questions.

Applying Past Knowledge to New Situations – This habit reminds us to learn from our past experiences and apply our knowledge to new experiences. Each of us has encountered many different problems throughout our lives, and when we reflect on how we were able to solve our past problems we may find that the skills and strategies we used in the past can apply to a new situation. Successful language learners know that knowledge of their first language can help with their second language through cognates, literacy and more.

Remaining Open to Continuous Learning - This habit encourages us to always keep an open mind and allow new information to change the way we think. We are reminded that nobody can possibly know everything there is to know, and even the oldest person in the world has something to learn. Every day gives us new opportunities to add to what we already know and become better problem solvers. Successful language learners know that there are always new words and expressions to learn and that it is okay not to know what something means and to ask for clarification.

Chapter 5
LAF while Listening with Understanding and Empathy & Thinking Interdependently

Although developing the habit of listening is a challenge, it is certainly one of the most teachable and most essential HoM to learn as early as possible. As lifelong learners, we know the value of listening, and yet we may find it quite difficult to listen to our own learners. After all, we have so much to say and share as teachers! Listening to our students automatically guarantees that we are not speaking, and that is quite difficult for some of us—myself included. We tend to think that we have heaps of valuable information to teach them; we know so much more of the language than they do! If they would only listen, then they could learn!

While it is certainly true that each of us will know more of the language we are teaching than will our learners, it is also true that by listening to them we will become better teachers and they will get more time to practice language in the classroom. When we give our students the chance to speak to us and to one another, and we truly listen to them with understanding and empathy, we can learn both from them and about them. We can learn what they need, what they want, their dreams, their frustrations and their passions. We can use this information to design better lessons and to make lessons more personal and meaningful for our learners. Listening gives us a window into the cultural perspectives that our students are coming to us with and allows us to connect with them on a level that goes beyond the surface.

As with all HoM, Listening with Understanding and Empathy and Thinking Interdependently take practice. With all learners, listening needs to be reinforced daily, and, fortunately, it can be employed anywhere. This type of listening is beyond what we normally consider listening. It is not only hearing what the other person is saying and keeping quiet so that he or she can say it, but also relating to what the other person is saying by trying to understand that person's perspective. It implies that we are willing as listeners to put ourselves in the shoes of the person who is talking to us. We become open to understanding other perspectives, and willing to put aside our own perspectives momentarily, or adapt our own perspective through our interactions with others. Listening with empathy and understanding is an active and creative process.

True Stories of TESOL

Let me tell you a story about one of my many teaching flops that demonstrates the importance of both Listening with Understanding and Empathy as well as Thinking Interdependently. I was a young teacher in Morocco working at the American Language Center in Casablanca. I had already worked as a bilingual teacher in California and as an EFL teacher in Costa Rica for several years before I got to Morocco, so I thought I knew a thing or two about teaching language. In addition, being one of the few teachers trained in TESOL where I worked, I was asked to provide some professional development much like I had done in Costa Rica. With all of this education and varied experience in my head, I thought I knew what I was doing as I began my semester teaching mostly adolescent and young adult language learners. I proceeded to prepare my lessons much like I had in Costa

Rica with learners of a similar age. I gathered the books and materials I needed to use in the classroom and began my semester. However, my lessons did not go as planned, not because my learners refused to interact or engage with the lessons, rather because I could not get them to stop talking.

You may think it is wonderful that my learners were so engaged and interactive in the classroom. After all, a language teacher's goal is, to a large extent, to get her learners to talk. It is true that my learners' energy and engagement in the classroom was exceptional. However, they were constantly talking about anything besides the task at hand. They were frequently off task and chatting about other things, often in Arabic or French, and I could not seem to get them to focus. This meant that the learning tasks I had designed often went unfinished. I was continuously being asked questions about myself and what was going on in my life during carefully planned cooperative learning activities that were meant to practice certain kinds of grammar and vocabulary. Thus, students were not getting the practice that they needed in English and were not progressing in a way that I could measure. Nothing was ever completed and I was very frustrated. I kept asking my learners to stay on task to complete their activities, and they would always cooperate for a few minutes, until somebody else thought of a question for me that would put the whole class off task again.

Finally, I complained about this phenomenon with one of my coworkers. He had been teaching in Morocco for some time, though he had no previous training or education in teaching language learners. His native English speaking ability is what had secured the position for him. This colleague informed me that the behavior I was experiencing from my students in the classroom was simply "the way Moroccans are." He said Moroccans were extremely sociable, and that is why the interactive activities I had been using would not work in the classroom. He recommended that I stick to grammar and vocabulary exercises in the book and cut down on trying any other kinds of activities. He said, "If you give them an inch, they'll take a mile, and then you get nothing done."

Talking to my colleague depressed me. I wondered if what he said could possibly be true and all of the knowledge I had accumulated about language acquisition and teaching through interactive strategies was going to go to waste in Morocco. I may have considered switching my teaching style for a second or two, but I knew it wasn't me. I could never do that. I would be a miserable teacher, and I feared my students would also be miserable. I decided to do something else. It was a little bit sneaky, but it worked. I played a trick on my students.

The next time I walked into the classroom, I began teaching exactly the way my colleague had told me I should. I asked the students to open their books and began to go over a grammar exercise straight from the book without trying to create any kind of interactive activity to accompany it. My classroom was silent. No talking at all, only one word answers to questions from the book, if any. I moved on to a fill-in-the-blank vocabulary activity from the book. That took up about half of the class time. As I went over the vocabulary activity with my students, I made sure not to expand on answers, ask follow up questions or give examples. I told no stories. The looks on my students' faces were a mixture of confusion and fear. They didn't know what had come over me. It was not the kind of classroom they were accustomed to with me. There was no laughing, no engagement, and basically no talking.

When we were done I asked the students to close their books. I then said something along the lines of, "Now we will be doing a listening exercise. I will tell you a story and you need to listen carefully. You may take notes. After the story I will ask you questions about what you heard." I proceeded to tell them the story of a young teacher who was enthusiastic about teaching language learners through fun activities but who was ultimately so frustrated by her learners not following directions and going off task that she resorted to teaching by doing book exercises and vocabulary memorization, and that it made her so sad that she decided to leave teaching and study another career. You may think the story was a bit dramatic. It was, but so am I. The story made my point in a way that my nagging at them during activities hadn't.

At first my students were listening carefully to my story and taking notes, but soon most of them began to realize I was telling a story about myself. My colleague in some senses was correct. Moroccan culture as a whole is a very sociable culture where people very much care about one another and are curious about each other. The students who realized that the story was about me immediately started saying, "No Teacher!" and "We love how you teach us!" This story helped me express to them how I felt and opened up a listening session for all of us.

I spent the rest of class that day listening to my students with understanding and empathy, just as they had listened to me. I heard from them how they felt about the class and how they wanted the class to proceed. We then broke into small groups to think interdependently about how to make the class work in ways that met their need to socialize as well as their language acquisition needs. They came up with some great ideas and we finally arrived at a decision. Every class would begin with a five-minute catch up session where we would share any news we wanted to with one another in English. This would be followed by story time. They wanted me to tell them a story every class about my experiences in Morocco or in other places as a learner or teacher. They all agreed that my stories were very important to them and they enjoyed listening and asking questions. After that we would do the activities I prepared and stay on task until they were done. And it worked! Following this listening intervention, my class was largely cooperative and my students were able to complete tasks, learning much of what I had planned for them to learn. Once in a while when things would start to go off track, I would make comments such as, "I'm thinking about quitting teaching and opening a café." This would cause a few smiles and chuckles, an apology, and they would go back to focusing on the learning task.

This situation provided an opportunity for me to teach students how to listen to me with empathy and understanding. I hadn't done that when I was simply trying to redirect them during learning tasks. I had not bothered to speak to them from the heart about my concerns. I also learned to listen with understanding and empathy to their needs and to work together while thinking interdependently with them to resolve the issue. In this way, I was able to meet both their need to socialize as well as their need to acquire English in ways that matched my teaching style. We all benefitted.

Techniques for the Classroom

One specific technique for listening with empathy and understanding/thinking interdependently that I developed with my learners in Morocco (and still use) is a 'listening circle.' This is an invisible circle that surrounds us when it is time to take a listening break. In that circle each of us can express whatever he or she needs to say without interruption and without any technological interference such as cell phones, tablets and computers. Our rules are that we look at the one who is speaking, don't interrupt or judge, and do our best to understand. This is a special space that is created at some point during our learning journey, usually once a week, to make sure we are all on track. When I have a classroom of language learners, I lead and model the listening circle for them several times before asking them if they would like to lead a listening circle with a topic of concern to them as students in the classroom. The listening circles I have had in my classes have given me more insight into the needs and wants of my learners than any other activities I have done, but this is only achieved after there is an atmosphere of trust and a lowering of the affective filter in the class.

Other ideas and activities for Listening with Understanding and Empathy, and Thinking Interdependently are described below. When you implement these techniques, you are modeling them for your learners and teaching their usefulness as well. I like to point them out sometimes, though not always, to show my learners what I am doing and to encourage them to do the same. I give them the words for each part of listening and when I see them do the same with me or with one another, I acknowledge that they have done so and praise them. This helps to both enhance their vocabulary and acknowledge their efforts to develop the HoM.

Pausing, Paraphrasing & Probing

1. **Pausing**—Encourage your language learners to talk by not jumping in and interrupting them (this can be difficult), and make sure they know you are interested and empathetic by giving them a chance to think after you ask a question or during a conversation. Embrace silence; you don't have to fill every second of a conversation. In teaching we call this silence 'wait time.' It is a skill that new teachers are encouraged to develop. In my own teaching at the university level as well as with my language learners, I have developed a little trick that forces me to wait for a reply to my question or comment rather than jumping in to answer or ask another question. I hum the theme song to the game show *Jeopardy!* in my head while I am waiting. I have found that this amount of time is ideal in giving my students the chance to develop a response even when it seems that none may be forthcoming. For language learners wait time is especially necessary. They need more time to formulate a response in their heads than do native speakers. When we are teaching mixed classes of language learners and native speakers, it is especially important to clarify for all students that waiting is an act of support and empathy for language learners.

2. **Paraphrasing**—After you listen to your learners, paraphrase what they have said to make sure you understand, and to model for them how to say what they are trying to say in the target language. You can begin your sentence with, "So, you are saying…," or, "So, you are worried about…." This 'so,… technique' shows that you are not just listening, but you are listening with empathy by putting yourself in your learners' shoes. This technique ensures that learners will know that you are trying to understand them and help them improve their language. It is important not to pass judgment when you are paraphrasing, even if the learner is expressing an opinion you don't agree with or is contrary to what you are trying to teach. When listening with empathy it is also helpful to label the feeling. Using statements such as, "You're frustrated because…" or, "You're worried because…" can be a helpful and positive way to paraphrase.

3. **Probing**—When you hear your learners make a general statement such as, "This is too hard, I can't do it," ask probing questions to help them clarify their ideas, and show you are listening and creating empathy. For example, you could respond by asking, "What is hard for you about this exercise?" Keep asking questions to narrow down the topic, to show you care, are trying to understand, and are committed to helping them learn. When learners start to gain confidence with a new language, become more adept at thinking about their own thinking and are encouraged to be reflective, their abilities to understand themselves, make themselves understood and solve the problems they encounter along the way will be strongly enhanced.

LAF in Class: Listening with Understanding and Empathy/Thinking Interdependently

1. Listening & Imagining

Language Skill Focus	Listening and writing
Language Functions Practiced	Explaining, describing, listening to others, asking questions
Grammar/Vocabulary Practiced	Simple present tense, present continuous, descriptive adjectives Vocabulary will include words associated with the listening prompt. If you are using words you think your learners do not know, be sure to have a word bank and teach those words beforehand. It is better to use a prompt that is easily understood by learners at their comprehensible input level.
Grouping Strategy	Individual, whole group
LAF Aspects	<ul><li>Personal and meaningful: Learners are expressing their own ideas.</li><li>Cooperative: When learners work in pairs or when they build on one another's ideas during interaction.</li><li>Engaging: Learners are engaged in the story and listening in order to complete the task.</li><li>Interactive: Learners share their ideas and interact while being questioned by the teacher.</li><li>Values diversity: Learners demonstrate different perspectives with their responses.</li><li>Higher order thinking: With more than one right answer, learners must think abstractly and consider various possibilities in order to complete the activity. They can be creative and analytical in their responses.</li></ul>
Primary HoM Practiced	Listening with Understanding and Empathy, Thinking Interdependently, Communicating with Clarity and Precision
Materials Needed	Text that paints a picture with words, paper and pencil

STEPS

- Ask learners to close their eyes and visualize while you read a descriptive paragraph from a book, or make up a scene of your own. [An example scene is provided below.]
- Tell learners that they will be answering questions about the scene that they imagine. Emphasize that there is more than one right answer to each question.
- Read the paragraph or scene twice.
- Have learners number a paper from one to five.
- Ask learners five questions about the passage you just read.
- Ask questions that can have multiple correct answers rather than only one factual answer. For example, if you are reading a passage about a forest, ask a question about what kinds of trees there are in the forest, the kinds of noises that can be heard there, etc.

Sample Scene with associated questions:

I'm driving to work on a very hot day and I am stuck in traffic. I see some children playing in the backseat of a car next to me on my left. I see a couple who seem to be arguing in the car on my right. There is a man walking between cars selling food and drinks. I can hear music blasting from the car in front of me.

Questions:
1. What month do you think this is?
2. What are the children playing in the car?
3. What kind of food and drinks is the man selling?
4. What type of music is playing?
5. What is the couple arguing about?

Below is a transcribed example from adult language learners who participated in this activity. You can see how they answered the questions with their developing language skills. Notice how I error correct them through modeling the 'correct' way to give the response in English without stopping the conversation. Many times the learners will self-correct as they listen to the correct language usage being modeled. L=Learner, T = Teacher

Q1:   What month do you think it is?
       L: Hot so is July.
       T: So, because it is hot, you think it is probably July?
       L: Yes, hot so is July.
       T: It's hot so it's July?
       L: Yes, it's hot, so it's July.
       L2: Or maybe August also.
       T: So, it could be August.
       L2: It could be August.

Q2:   What are the children playing in the car?
       L: Childrens is playing the game of the hands.
       T: The children are playing a game with their hands?
       L: Yes, is playing a game with the hands.
       T: So, the children are playing a clapping game like this? (demonstrate)
       L: No, are playing like this. (demonstrates)

T: Ok, so the children are playing a hand game like this…

L: Yes, the children are playing a hand game.

T: Anybody else?

L2: The children are playing the cards?

T: They're playing cards?

Q3: What kind of food and drinks is the man selling?

L1: Coke and candy.

L2: Water and candy.

L3: Water and the sandwich.

T: The man is selling water and a sandwich?

L: Yes, water and a sandwich.

T: Just one sandwich or sandwiches?

L: Sandwiches.

T: So, the man is selling water and sandwiches?

L: Yes, water and sandwiches, also fruit.

Q4: What type of music is playing?

L: Music is the heavy.

T: The music is heavy metal?

L: Yes, heavy metal, very loud.

L2: Rock music.

L3: Loud music.

Q5: What is the couple arguing about?

L: The couple is the arguing about money.

T: They are arguing about money?

L: Yes, arguing about money.

L2: They has marriage problems.

T: They have marriage problems?

L2: Yes, they have marriage problems.

L3: The man has a girlfriend is not his wife.

L4: I think this too! I think the same.

T: Oh no, the man is having an affair?

L3: Yes, he is having an affair!

These answers illustrate that even when we hear the exact same scene, what we picture happening in our minds can be quite different. Listening activities such as this help learners to see how we can all have different perspectives even with the same information. It helps us to practice listening and see that listening is an active process that has as much to do with hearing as it does with perspective. By hearing one another's interpretations, we begin to develop empathy for one another and appreciate multiple perspectives.

For language learners, even at the lower levels, it is important for them to express their personal opinions and perspectives as much as possible. Activities that allow them to show their own personalities are essential.

Adaptations	<u>Make it easier</u> by modeling the activity first so that learners understand the task; and make the listening shorter and easier. <u>Make it harder</u> by using a longer passage that is more complicated and by doing less modeling. You can also make it even harder by restricting the possibilities in the answers by applying limitations. For example, you could require all answers to begin with the letter K, or instead of giving your answer when asked you need to give three clues for the class to guess what your answer is.
Remote Learning	This particular activity can easily be delivered remotely without any modifications.

2. Building on Ideas Together

Language Skill Focus	Speaking, listening
Language Functions Practiced	Expanding, describing, linking and connecting ideas
Grammar/Vocabulary Practiced	Simple present, simple past, modals, conditionals Vocabulary practiced will depend on the topic chosen; provide new vocabulary as needed in a word bank or other
Grouping Strategy	Individual, whole group
LAF Aspects	<ul><li>Personal and meaningful: Learners give their own personal ideas and thoughts.</li><li>Engaging: Learners generally enjoy building something together.</li><li>Repetition: The repetition in this activity is helpful for learners to practice language.</li><li>Interactive. There is no way to do this without interacting in the target language.</li><li>Cooperative. Learners need to cooperate by building on what others say.</li><li>Multicultural: Different perspectives are allowed and welcomed.</li><li>Higher order thinking: Learners must think abstractly to construct arguments.</li><li>Task based: Students are completing a structure together.</li></ul>
Primary HoM Practiced	Listening with Understanding and Empathy, Thinking Interdependently
Materials Needed	Legos, Lincoln logs or any other blocks/things that can be stacked or connected. As a variation, use a large piece of paper and markers or crayons.

STEPS

- Sit students in a circle or a square.
- Distribute building materials so that each learner has approximately the same number of objects.
- Explain that you will be doing a listening exercise where each person needs to build on what the previous person said.
- Use a topic that you think would be of interest to the learners.
- Begin a conversation about that topic with a starter 'springboard' sentence.
- For this activity, one person speaks at a time, incorporating what the person before said and building on it.
- At the same time, each person uses one of his or her building materials to connect to the building material of the person who just spoke.
- In this way a structure of some kind is created at the end of the activity.
- For example, if you have done a reading on something in the news, such as climate change, you could start your activity by saying something like, "I am worried about climate change but I don't know what to do about it." While saying this, you start the structure by putting your block, Lego or other object in the middle of the circle. The next person will build on this by saying something like, "I am worried about climate change too, I can stop using plastic bags when I shop." The learner adds a block while saying this, and so on.
- A variation on this activity is to have a large piece of paper and markers to create a cooperative design by the end of the activity that each person has contributed to.

Adaptations	<u>Make it easier</u> by keeping the initial reading or springboard short and contextual, and demanding only a word or two from each learner. For example, provide a short reading about people getting ready to go on a picnic followed by each person saying what they would bring along. 1. I am going to bring a blanket to sit on. 2. I am going to bring a blanket to sit on and a hat for the sun. 3. I am going to bring a blanket to sit on, a hat for the sun and water to drink. <u>Make it harder</u> by giving a more linguistically demanding reading or listening springboard, such as a short news video or article, and setting up a timer so that there is a very short amount of time allowed for each turn, making learners need to think and speak quickly. ● Make it easier by cutting down on the time each person is expected to speak, providing sentence stems and sentence starters such as the following: "I think that,…" "You said that…" "I agree because…" "I have a different perspective…." ● Make it harder by giving each speaker more time to elaborate on the topic so they have to fill that time with language, giving topics that are more challenging to talk about.
Remote Learning	This activity is more challenging to do remotely. You won't be able to build a physical structure together if you are not in the same location, but by using a remote tool that allows for a communal drawing, you can do this activity in a modified way that can be fun.

3. RASA Listeners

Language Skill Focus	Listening and speaking
Language Functions Practiced	Explaining, describing, giving opinions, asking for clarification, summarizing, analyzing, justifying
Grammar/Vocabulary Practiced	Modals, adjectives, past tense, conditionals Vocabulary depends on topics chosen, for lower levels word banks can be utilized.
Grouping Strategy	Individual and whole group
LAF Aspects	Personal and meaningful: Learners give their own opinions and thoughts. Engaging: Learners generally enjoy talking about controversial topics. Interactive: There is no way to do this without interacting. Cooperative: They must listen and cooperate to complete the activity. Values diversity. Different perspectives are allowed and welcomed. Higher-order thinking: Learners must think abstractly to construct arguments. Task-based: There is a specific task that learners are being asked to complete.
Primary HoM Practiced	Listening with Understanding and Empathy, Thinking Interdependently, Communicating with Clarity and Precision
Materials Needed	None essential, soft background music and comfortable seating recommended

The acronym RASA is a term coined by Julian Treasure, an expert on listening. His TED Talks on listening have been helpful to me as a parent and teacher and I encourage you to watch them and listen to them carefully for more listening based teaching ideas https://www.ted.com/talks/julian_treasure_5_ways_to_listen_better?language=en.
The word 'rasa' is the Sanskrit word for 'juice' or 'essence' and it works as a great acronym for learners to remember when practicing listening with understanding and empathy as they practice a new language.

RASA

Receive, meaning paying attention to the person
Appreciate, meaning making little noises like "hmm," "ok"
Summarize using the word "so"
Ask questions afterwards

STEPS

- Have students face one another. It is a nice idea to have soft music playing in the background such as the music you normally hear in a yoga class.
- Ask learners to choose the topics that they want to discuss from a set of somewhat 'controversial' topics that have been written on the board or on index cards. Learners can also come up with their own topics.
- Ask a volunteer language learner to begin by talking about the given topic for 30 seconds. This seems short, but 30 seconds actually feels like a long time when speaking in a second language. The other learner **Receives** this input.
- As the speaker is laying out her argument on the topic, the partner is looking at her and using body language and appreciative feedback noises to assure that listening is taking place. Model this for your learners. This is the **Appreciate** part.
- When the speaker has finished, the partner is given about 30 seconds to **Summarize** and **Ask** questions.
- Then another round of RASA listening ensues based on the questions asked and their responses.
- This continues with more sets of partners and different topics. I suggest using the strongest language learners as models with the teacher for a few rounds before putting the students in pairs together.
- Once everyone understands how the activity works, students can be separated into pairs and continue the activity together with different topics. It is a good idea to switch up the pairs every five minutes or so.
- Learners are encouraged to bring up any topic or issue that they would like to speak about. Make sure you explain to your learners that there is no real need to come to consensus or agreement on topics while using this technique; the idea is to be truly listened to, and to begin to form a path towards understanding that may take some time to navigate.

Possible Topics:

*Marriage   Vaccines   Cloning   Online Dating   AI
Animal Rights   Bed Times   Gun Rights   Homework
Climate Change   Plastic Surgery   Social Media   Death Penalty*

Adaptations	<u>Make it easier</u> by cutting down on the time each person is expected to speak, providing topics, sentence stems, and sentence starters such as the following: "I think that,…" "You said that…" "I agree because…" "I have a different perspective…." <u>Make it harder</u> by giving each speaker more time to elaborate on the topic so they have to fill that time with language, giving topics that are more challenging to talk about or having learners bring their own topics.
Remote Learning	This activity is easily adapted to the remote learning classroom. Be sure to model the process for your students ahead of time. A short prepared video would be a good way to do this. Learners can then proceed to do the activity in pairs in separate rooms, coming together to present to the whole class once they have practiced the activity in pairs. Teachers would visit each room to give support and scaffolding as needed.

4. Big Questions for the Universe

Focus On	Speaking and listening
Grouping Strategy	Whole group, individual, pair
Language Functions Practiced	Explaining, hypothesizing, agreeing, disagreeing, giving opinions, contradicting, supporting
Grammar/Vocabulary Practiced	Declaratives, modals, simple present, conditionals Vocabulary is ependent on the big questions chosen. The teacher can provide readings related to questions for vocabulary support.
Grouping Strategy	Whole group, individual, pair
LAF Aspects	<ul><li>Personal and meaningful: Learners are expressing their own ideas and asking their own questions.</li><li>Engaging: Learners are actively engaged in using language.</li><li>Uses visuals: Graphics may be used to accompany questions and provide context.</li><li>Interactive: Learners interact with one another to complete the task by discussing their ideas.</li><li>Cooperative: Learners cooperate by exchanging papers.</li><li>Repetition: There is repetition as they explain their ideas.</li><li>Higher order thinking: Learners have to come up with a their own answers to big questions.</li><li>Values diversity: Different ways of understanding and interpreting the world are part of the activity.</li></ul>
Primary HoM Practiced	Listening with Understanding and Empathy, Thinking Interdependently, Questioning and Problem Posing, Striving for Accuracy, Thinking Flexibly
Materials Needed	Websites or books that feature big philosophical or ethical questions created for thinking and learning. One of these is Operation Meditation (operationmeditation.com) but there are many others. Paper and something to write with, or journals to record thoughts and ideas.

This activity starts with the selection of a Big Question. You can have these questions on index cards stored in an index card file or simply come up with them one at a time as you do this activity. I find it helpful to have a picture file, a question file, and an activity folder where I keep activities that I can grab and use any time with minimal preparation or materials needed. As a teacher, I began to accumulate pictures many years ago and now have a nice collection of pictures that I have mounted on cardstock, and that I can add to whenever I am so inclined. Similarly, when I invent or adapt activities, I often put the directions and whatever materials I need for the activity in a manila envelope. I keep activity envelopes in folders that I can throw in my bag on my way to a class. For my Big Questions for the Universe activity, I keep a question file that includes questions I have found or created, and questions that have been given to me by my learners. Some of these questions are listed below:

- What is gravity?
- Why are we here?
- Is the 'self' an illusion?
- Where were we before we were born?
- How can numbers go on forever?
- Is there an end to the universe?
- What is truth?
- Why do people hurt each other?
- Does everybody have the same feelings?
- What are thoughts?
- Is there intelligent life on another planet in another galaxy?
- Is freedom more important than love?
- What is love?
- What is freedom?
- Is there a purpose to life?
- Is meaning arbitrary?
- Do animals think?
- Will humans become extinct?

As you can see, these questions have no easy answers and are highly philosophical in nature. This activity allows learners the freedom to ask questions of themselves and of one another without the obligation of coming up with a final or correct answer in the end. Some learners will need to be convinced that this ambiguity is okay or else they will feel frustrated with the exercise. The idea is that the learners are practicing language while they are exploring concepts and using their critical thinking skills.

STEPS

- Choose a Big Question from your question file.
- Once the question is chosen by whatever means you come up with, read the question to your learners, asking them to listen carefully.
- Next, give one full timed minute to just think about the question. Do not allow any writing or talking during this thinking time.
- Once the minute is over, give a five full minutes to free write on the question.
- Have learners pair up and read their responses to one another. Encourage learners

to listen carefully, respond to one another with empathy and include questions for clarification.

- As a variation, have learners exchange papers and write interactive comments to one another.
- An interactive comment implies that an interaction will follow, so it is usually a question or an insight on what was written that invites further discussion. I model this for my students when I write interactive comments on their writing so that they know how to do it by the time we get to this activity.
- Once each student has either spoken and responded with a partner, or written and received an interactive comment, a whole class discussion can follow.
- There are endless directions that this activity can take after that, including doing online research on the topic, creating a piece of artwork or music to represent the ideas generated by the question, and many more.
- A variation on this activity is asking the question and then having the students find an image or an object to represent the question, with a discussion to follow.
- Yet another variation is having students come up with five additional questions based on the original question and playing a 'one minute to answer' game where questions are asked and answered quickly followed by a more thoughtful discussion.

The following is an example of a free write followed by an interactive comment. This example is from a young teen learner.

Big Question: What is love?

Free Write: *When I think about love, I think about the way I feel when I love another person. I feel like I want to be with that person, that I want that person to be happy and safe. I think that love is almost like a gravitational pull towards another person, it is an attraction like a magnet that you can't see but that you can feel. Like a hug from the Earth. Of course some magnets are stronger than others and you can be pulled in many directions at the same time with love.*

Interactive Comment: *So you talk about the feeling that you are being pulled towards a person but what about when that person doesn't love you back? Why does something that feels so strong and right end up hurting us sometimes?*

Big questions are an important part of giving learners a chance to question and problem pose while concurrently practicing language, thinking creatively and flexibly, practicing metacognition, and responding with wonderment and awe.

Adaptations	<u>Make it easier</u> by starting this as a whole class discussion where you model the kinds of answers that might be pertinent to example questions, letting learners listen to one another's ideas and writing these on the board. <u>Make it harder</u> by giving little or no examples and giving learners less time to think and write their responses. By adding extension activities you can also increase the challenge, as well as give learners vocabulary that they must weave into their responses.
Remote Learning	This activity can easily be adapted to remote learning without any special modifications.

5. Thinking/Feeling Cubes

Language Skill Focus	Listening and speaking
Language Functions Practiced	Explaining, describing, listening to others, asking questions
Grammar/Vocabulary Practiced	Interrogatives, past & present tense Vocabulary can include feeling words such as: sad, happy, angry, confused, frustrated, surprised, shocked, overjoyed, thrilled, excited, furious, curious…
Grouping Strategy	Individual and whole group
LAF Aspects	• Personal and meaningful: Learners are expressing their own feelings. • Engaging: Learners are involved in making something that takes the focus off language. • Interactive: Learners are interacting with a teacher and one another as they flip cubes. • Purposeful: A product (cube) is created that serves a purpose in the classroom. • Values diversity: Learners demonstrate different perspectives visually. • Task based: Learners must complete a specific task.
Primary HoM Practiced	Listening with Understanding & Empathy, Thinking Flexibly, Gathering Data Through all the Senses, Managing Impulsivity
Materials Needed	Square cardboard boxes (such as tissue boxes), construction paper or regular paper, markers, crayons, old magazines, glue and scissors. Optional: The picture book, The Rabbit Listened by Cori Doerrfield

STEPS

- Tell your learners a short story about a time when you felt that nobody was listening to you, or find a story online or in a book about the same thing. If you have the book, The Rabbit Listened, this is a wonderful picture book to use with language learners because it brings the idea home of the need to be listened to with very few words.
- Make sure that learners understand by doing comprehension checks, using body language, visuals that might help clarify meaning, and encouraging learners to ask you questions about the experience.
- Ask learners to brainstorm about a time when they weren't being listened to and to draw a picture of how that felt.
- Show learners a listening/feeling cube that you have already constructed as a model.
- Instruct learners to create listening/feeling cubes by giving directions that lead to covering a square box with paper and drawing different feelings on the four sides of the box.
- For example, your learner might draw a happy face on one side, a sad face on another, an angry and a frustrated face on the other two sides of the box. This is the 'feeling' part.
- On the top and bottom of the box have learners illustrate different techniques for paying attention and understanding one another, such as an eye and an ear for seeing and listening.
- Ask your learners to show you what side of the box they want you to see during lessons. Do they want you to know they are sad, or angry? They can show you by pointing that side of the box your way rather than speaking when they do not feel inclined to speak. Do they need you to listen more carefully or look at them? They can point that side of the box your way.
- You can also use your own box to give them the visual cue they might need during your interactions.

This project incorporates art, kinesthetic learning, and listening with empathy into a task-based activity that most learners will enjoy and that can be used throughout lessons. It is normally an activity that is done with younger learners but can also be done with older learners who struggle with expressing themselves, or during a lesson that involves a reading or video with a lot of emotions.

Adaptations	<u>Make it easier</u> by giving lower level language learners more modeling and context by increasing the body language and gestures used in explanations. Feelings are often expressed through facial gestures and body language, and this can be a way to engage learners kinesthetically. <u>Make it harder</u> by adding less common emotions and feelings to the repertoire of your learners through new vocabulary or short descriptions of situations that they can come up with emotions for. Instead of a cube, they can construct an object with more sides or a poster to fill in more potential emotions.
Remote Learning	In a remote learning classroom, your students will probably not have access to the materials needed to build a cube. However, they do have access to emojis and other online symbols and graphics that can be used. You can ask them to build up a set of emojis or other visuals that express feelings that they can add to their user names and switch out during lessons. This can give you a visual cue of where your learners are emotionally.

Chapter 6
LAF while Persisting & Managing Impulsivity

Persisting and Managing Impulsivity are two Habits of Mind that many of us struggle with. Who among us doesn't have moments of distraction that interrupt focus, situations where we overreact, or impulsive decisions that we later regret? Who hasn't wanted to catch a word or a phrase that has escaped from your mouth and stuff it right back in? It can be difficult not to feel like giving up at such times. It can be especially challenging to keep plugging away at difficult tasks, such as language learning, when the stakes are high and the progress is slow. At times, the persistence that is required to stick with the daily task of language learning can seem almost impossible. The frustration we might feel at repeated failures in our language learning journey can easily lead to difficulty in managing impulsivity and to a rejection of the persistence that is required for such a large task.

My own journey as a language learner and teacher of language learners has been fraught with experiences revolving around persistence and managing impulsivity. I have felt the need to manage my own impulsivity and encourage my learners to manage theirs on a daily basis. At the same time, while I am very good at starting projects, I am not good at all at finishing them. I have started at least 10 novels that remain incomplete at different stages, not to mention countless articles and household projects. I have started teaching myself guitar at least a dozen times, only to give up after a few weeks. I clearly have trouble with persisting.

Once I learned about these two important HoM, I knew I had to find ways to incorporate these concepts into my teaching, as much for my students as for myself. I have found that modeling the HoM for our students is one important way to practice them ourselves.

True Stories in TESOL

One of my bilingual kindergarteners once taught me a valuable lesson about both persistence and managing impulsivity. Xochitl was a five-year-old Mexican American girl, the daughter of migrant workers in Salinas, California. Xochitl's family members had numerous economic and social challenges that did not allow them to give her the support she needed to practice the many things we were learning that year in school. Consequently, although she was very bright, she lagged behind her classmates in some of the skill areas learned in kindergarten. Yet, Xochitl was determined to learn.

Whenever I asked for a volunteer, Xochitl was the first to raise her hand and offer to help. She did everything with gusto, even those things she did not do well, and she never stopped trying. One day I overheard another child telling her that she was the only one in the class who didn't know how to write her own name by herself. I was about to take the child aside and explain why that wasn't a very nice thing to say when I heard Xochitl respond, "I'll do it when I'm ready. I need more practice." I stopped in my tracks. Xochitl clearly understood her own needs and had her own timeline.

I had been helping Xochitl write her name when she was taking too long, so she could rejoin the class. Xochitl's words reminded me to give her the time she needed. I learned to be okay with her missing some activities so she could keep practicing others at her own pace. By the end of the year Xochitl was writing her name beautifully, with extra swirls, and just about at the same level as the other kids. If I had continued to let my own teacher impulsivity take over, to try to hurry up her learning, I would not have been giving her the time and space she needed to let her persistence and patience lead to success.

Techniques for the Classroom

Managing Impulsivity and Persistence promote the values of reflection, focus, grit, and composure. Language learners who learn to apply these HoM to their language acquisition journey have a major advantage over those who don't. These learners are more likely to be patient with themselves, to carefully read directions, to ask for help when they are frustrated, and to not give up. Bright language learners who don't apply these HoM may never achieve the language level that they are capable of.

One strategy originally created by a school using the Habits of Mind (Costa & Kallick, 2008) includes using STAR rewards for kids who manage their impulsivity. This strategy can also serve language learners at any age. STAR is an acronym that stands for Stop, Think, Act, and Reflect. We can teach this to our learners and practice using it on a daily basis, both during learning time and at other times when managing impulsivity is necessary. During those situations we can do the following:

- **Stop:** take a deep breath or two, and don't react immediately.
- **Think**: What is going on? Label the problem and the feelings. What just happened and what are my choices? Ask questions if necessary.
- **Act:** make a thoughtful decision about what to do and put it in to action.
- **Reflect:** Was what I did a good idea? Could I have done something differently and obtained a better result?

Other ways to put this HoM into action include practicing visualization of different reactions after a moment of stress in the classroom, role playing with learners on how to react during times of stress and frustration, and using journaling and creative expression to explore feelings and reactions. All of these strategies can help, but none will work if not practiced regularly over time with plenty of patience and lots of imagination.

LAF in Class: Activities with Managing Impulsivity & Persisting

1. Good Idea/Bad Idea

Language Skill Focus	Listening and speaking
Language Functions Practiced	Explaining, describing, making propositions, giving consequences, persuading
Grammar/Vocabulary Practiced	Simple present, simple past, past continuous, adjectives; vocabulary depends on situations chosen
Grouping Strategy	Pairs
LAF Aspects	• Personal and meaningful: Learners get to use their own toys if they are little and make up their own situations. • Engaging: Learners generally enjoy this activity because it is hands on and fun. • Interactive: There is no way to do this without interacting. • Cooperative: They must cooperate in pairs to complete the activity. • Repetition: There is natural repetition during this activity. • Higher order thinking: Learners must think of how to resolve different scenarios. • Values diversity: A variety of perspectives and possibilities are welcome and encouraged.
Primary HoM Practiced	Managing Impulsivity, Persisting, Listening with Understanding and Empathy, Thinking Interdependently, Thinking Flexibly, Finding Humor

Materials Needed	For younger learners, dolls, stuffed animals, action figures or puppets can be used. For older learners these items are not necessary but they can still be used for fun. Older learners can take on the roles themselves or you can give learners nametags to represent their role. For example, a nametag that says BOSS or EMPLOYEE. The picture book, That is NOT a good idea by Mo Willems is a fun book to read with learners. It has very few words and many images that give context and a twist on the "good idea/bad idea" theme.

STEPS

- Give learners nametags with role names such as SERVER and CUSTOMER for a role-playing activity. Give younger learners dolls, stuffed animals, action figures or puppets to use.
- Remind learners of the meaning of Managing Impulsivity with a description and some examples. You may find it helpful to tell them an anecdote about a time when you had trouble managing your own impulsivity.
- Ask learners to share an anecdote of their own.
- Have younger learners use their toys to role-play good idea/bad idea. They do this by being presented with a situation where their toys have to make a choice and either manage their impulsivity or not, demonstrating good ideas vs. bad ideas.
- For example, teddy may want to eat all of the cookies made by Barbie because he is very hungry. He either has to control himself and eat only one so that he can share with all of the other toys or he has to give in to his impulsivity and devour them all.
- For older learners you could have a restaurant scenario where a customer feels that the food is not well cooked or any other conflict scenario.
- Start by saying, "bad idea" first. Younger learners generally have fun with their toys making bad choices. For example, teddy might eat all the cookies and get a tummy ache. In the older learner restaurant scenario, a bad idea might be to insult the server, storm out of the restaurant or throw the plate.
- Next, say, "good idea," and see how learners manage their impulsivity. Teddy may need some strategies to control himself, such as looking away or asking for a drink of water.
- Be sure to model how to show a good and a bad idea beforehand so learners get the hang of it and then let their imaginations run wild.
- The scenarios you choose can come from issues you know your learners are struggling with in real life, situations from your class readings or learner's own created scenarios.

Adaptations	<u>Make it easier:</u> You can prepare several example dialogues to begin the activity where you give students the actual words to use and the turn taking for making their choices. The first dialogue can include all the words, while the second and third can have many words left out that they need to fill in with their own ideas. Providing a word bank here is helpful. Once students are comfortable, you can have them do this with no dialogues at all. <u>Make it harder:</u> Give students a variety of tricky situations that they need to resolve with less modeling. An alternative is to have students create their own scenarios from things that have actually happened to them, things they saw in movies or books, or things that they create on their own.
Remote Learning	This activity is easily adapted to remote learning by first modeling the activity, then providing the support needed and separating students into pairs or small cooperative groups of four and having them work on their scenarios. This can be done in separate remote rooms. Make sure to visit each room to provide support and guidance to the students. After enough time has passed for groups to come up with at least one scenario, bring the whole group back together for a virtual performance, or have students record their group time and play it for the whole class.

2. Explosions

Language Skill Focus	Listening and speaking
Language Functions Practiced	Explaining, describing, making propositions, giving consequences, persuading
Grammar/Vocabulary Practiced	Simple past, past continuous, present perfect; vocabulary depends on topics chosen by student and includes the vocabulary of the springboard readings
Grouping Strategy	Pairs and whole group, individual extensions
LAF Aspects	<ul><li>Personal and meaningful: Learners get to use their own toys if they are little and make up their own situations.</li><li>Engaging: Learners generally enjoy this activity because it is hands on and fun.</li><li>Interactive: There is no way to do this without interacting.</li><li>Cooperative: They must cooperate in pairs to complete the activity.</li><li>Repetition: There is natural repetition during this activity.</li><li>Higher order thinking: Learners must think of how to resolve different scenarios.</li><li>Values diversity: A variety of perspectives and possibilities are welcome and encouraged.</li></ul>
Primary HoM Practiced	Managing Impulsivity, Persisting, Listening with Understanding & Empathy, Thinking Interdependently, Thinking Flexibly
Materials Needed	For younger learners, the picture book <u>My Mouth is a Volcano</u>! By Julia Cook, or any other book that talks about impulse control through an engaging (not a preachy) story. If you can't find a book, create your own story based on your own experiences or look for a free online story such as: "Bad Temper" http://www.english-for-students.com/Bad-Temper.html).

STEPS

- Read the selected story or reading to your learners, or have them read it themselves if they are able to do so. In the story of the volcano mouth, the main character has a very hard time managing his impulsivity. He blames his volcano mouth for the interruptions rather than taking the blame himself.
- In the bad temper story, a boy who often loses his temper is given a bag of nails. He needs to hammer one nail into a fence every time he loses his temper.
- Follow up on the reading with a short discussion of the events in the story and ideas on how to manage impulsivity.
- Have learners rewrite the story in pairs having the main characters make different choices and/or be confronted with different consequences.
- Learner pairs may act out their new version of the story for the whole class, or exchange written versions and act each other's versions out.
- As a follow up with younger learners, I have them do the yoga pose 'volcano' and self-erupt. In this pose, kids begin standing with their legs together and their hands at their sides. They then 'erupt' by jumping up, spreading their legs and raising their arms over their heads in an imitation of lava bursting out of a volcano. You can have them shout out things they sometimes feel like saying when they are frustrated or angry, such as "I am angry!" or "I am furious!" Teach your learners that when they are feeling pressure to 'erupt' they can always do a few volcano poses to get some energy out and manage their impulsivity.
- Older learners may also enjoy using body language or movement to express anger. Be aware of your own learners and what kinds of activities appeal to them.
- Extend the activity by having learners write and illustrate mini books of events in their lives where they were able, or not able, to manage their impulsivity.

Adaptations	Make it easier: Provide plenty of context by giving students visual representations of the readings. If you do not use a picture book, you can find images online that reflect the situation of the story. Make sure to use your own body language and facial gestures to enhance comprehensibility.
	Make it harder: Give less support and scaffolds to students as you read the story or as they read the chosen story on their own. Ask them to describe in more detail situations and solutions related to managing impulsivity or put together short role plays or dialogues to demonstrate past events.

Remote Learning	This activity is easily adapted to remote learning by reading to your students beforehand, then giving them time to come up with their own scenarios and ideas. Be sure to brainstorm with them as a whole group before having them go off on their own or in pairs to communicate their ideas. Good remote tools to use for this activity that are interactive include Nearpod and VoiceThread.

3. If it is to be, it's up to me

Language Skill Focus	Writing, reading, listening & speaking
Language Functions Practiced	Describing, predicting, suggesting
Grammar/Vocabulary Practiced	Simple past, past continuous, present perfect, modals; vocabulary depends on topics chosen
Grouping Strategy	Individual, pair, whole group
LAF Aspects	<ul><li>Personal and meaningful: Learners get to talk about themselves, their goals and their challenges.</li><li>Engaging: Learners stay involved because they are discussing what is important to them.</li><li>Interactive: Learners interact with one another as well as with the teacher.</li><li>Cooperative: They must cooperate in pairs to complete the activity.</li><li>Repetition: There is repetition and restating as they describe their partner's goals.</li><li>Higher order thinking: Learners must think of critically about their goals as well as their partner's goals.</li><li>Values diversity: A variety of perspectives and possibilities are a natural consequence of this activity.</li></ul>
Primary HoM Practiced	Persisting, Listening with Understanding & Empathy, Thinking Interdependently, Thinking Flexibly
Materials Needed	Paper, something to write with

STEPS

- Describe something that you achieved through persistence, or something that you would have liked to achieve but did not, due to lack of persistence.
- Ask learners to volunteer examples of something that they were able to achieve due to persistence. Collect some of these ideas on the board in a semantic web.
- Write the saying, "If it is to be, it's up to me," and ask learners to explain what that means to one another in pairs. Ask for volunteers to explain to whole group and give examples, making sure that everyone understands the meaning.
- Ask learners if they agree with the statement. Discuss why sometimes this is true and sometimes this is false. Write any key vocabulary words on the board for students to refer to.
- Have learners spend one to two minutes thinking of a goal that they would like to achieve that demands persistence. There should be no writing during this time.
- Have learners write their goal for about two minutes, including visuals if needed/wanted. Do not have students write their names on the paper.
- Collect papers and redistribute to the class so each learner receives the paper of a different learner.
- Ask students to read one another's written goals, and reply in writing with suggestions, tips and strategies for how to meet the goal.
- Put learners in pairs to discuss the goals they read and the suggestions they come up with. Have them brainstorm more suggestions together.
- Have learners share the goal they read and suggestions they come up with to class without reading from their papers.
- Ask the class to guess whose goal was read. The person whose goal it is should not give it away. Have class members add any additional tips or suggestions.
- You may also want to create a chart or semantic web on the board to group similar goals and similar strategies for maintaining persistence.

Adaptations	Make it easier: Do this as a whole class first. Tell students about your goal using plenty of context and body language as well as writing key words on the board. Write out your goal, and ask them to brainstorm tips for you. Write these out as models on the board. Give students more time to write, read and respond. Provide sentence starters for tips such as: You should… You could… Make it harder: After students complete the activity for themselves, ask them to think of a famous historical figure or living person and write a goal for them. Each student can read the goal aloud and the others can give suggestions and guess who the famous person or historical figure is. This can be based on what has been learned in class to tie in with content learning.
Remote Learning	This activity can be adapted for remote learning by completing the first part as you would in the classroom, and having students complete the part where they write their goals individually and submit them to the teacher. Teachers would then redistribute goals and have students write their responses before putting pairs in rooms to discuss. To facilitate this process, the explanation and initial whole group activity can be done in one lesson, and the goal writing can be done for homework.

4. Strip Stories

Language Skill Focus	Reading, listening and speaking
Language Functions Practiced	Repeating, making suggestions, asking for clarification, giving directions, expressing opinions
Grammar/Vocabulary Practiced	Dependent on the content of the story that is chosen for the activity. You can choose a story or reading that uses the vocabulary and/or grammar you wish to review.
Grouping Strategy	Individual, whole group
LAF Aspects	<ul><li>Personal and meaningful: Stories should have a connection to learners.</li><li>Engaging: Learners stay actively involved because they must do so to complete the activity.</li><li>Interactive: Learners interact with one another throughout the activity.</li><li>Cooperative: They must cooperate to complete the activity.</li><li>Repetition: There is repetition and restating constantly throughout the activity.</li><li>Higher order thinking: Learners must think critically about how to construct the story.</li><li>Values diversity: A variety of perspectives and possibilities for completing the activity are possible.</li></ul>
Primary HoM Practiced	Persisting, Managing Impulsivity, Thinking Interdependently, Thinking Flexibly
Materials Needed	Story or reading that is being used cut into strips of one sentence each. Ideally there is one strip for each learner, and stories or readings ideally should not be longer than 15 sentences. If you have more students, some can act as observers and directors to help the others along, or you can split the class into two groups, or add or delete sentences to create the right amount.

Strip stories are among my favorite activities for language learners. They are always interactive, challenging and fun. Not only do the learners practice the language that is found in the story, but they also generate a great deal of language themselves as they work out the solution together and complete the activity. Another great thing about strip stories is that they can be done with any story or reading that is relevant to your students, with small adaptations for length. This can include readings from your curriculum, or sections of larger readings and books.

STEPS

- Choose or create a short story or reading to work with; ideally the length will provide one sentence for each of your learners. If you need to add or delete sentences to get one sentence for each learner, do so without changing the logic of the story.
- Cut the story into strips so that each learner gets one strip.
- Sit learners in a circle.
- Distribute strips to the learners, making make sure you are not passing them out in the order they occur in the story!
- Have learners memorize exactly what is on their strip of paper – no writing allowed!
- Collect all of the pieces of paper.
- Tell learners that they each have one sentence of a story or reading and that they need to figure out how to put it together in the right order. No writing allowed. (Writing makes it much easier and cuts down on the language interaction they have while trying to figure out how to put the story together.)
- Learners may ask you how they should proceed, but it is important to tell them that they have to figure it out on their own, however they would like, but without writing.
- Learners will often start to say their sentences randomly, then start to move around or change seats. One or more learners may decide to take the initative and start directing the activity.
- Depending on how difficult it is to put the story together, learners will repeat their strips many times in order to listen to one another and figure out the story order.
- Occasionally, a learner will completely forget their sentence, or change their sentence significantly. If this happens, let learner see the original strip again. Do not say their sentence out loud; only the learner should see it.

Example Strip Story: Thomas Edison and Persistence

One day a little boy came home from school with a note in his pocket.

His mother read the note carefully.

It was from the boy's teacher.

"Your Tommy is too stupid to learn, take him out of school," it said.

The note angered the boy's mother, but she managed her temper.

She knew the teacher's opinion was wrong.

But what could she do if the teacher felt that way?

After thinking about it for a few minutes, she came to a decision.

She would teach Tommy herself, at home.

And that is exactly what she did.

Even though he had only three months of formal schooling in his life, the boy grew up to be a great inventor.

His name was Thomas Edison.

He invented many important things, including the light bulb and the phonograph.

Edison knew how important persistence was to being an inventor.

He is quoted as having said, "Genius is one percent inspiration and 99 percent perspiration".

Adaptations	<u>Make it easier</u> by offering a simple story or reading with clear transition words that show an order such as *first, then, next, finally*, etc. Another way to make it easier is to allow learners to maintain their strips of paper in hand. Another option is for the teacher to give hints and some direction. <u>Make it harder</u> by offering a more complex story or reading without clear transitions, or where a variety of orders is possible. Enforce a strict time limit.
Remote Learning	Strip stories would be difficult to do remotely but could be attempted. The teacher would need to give each learner a sentence privately then maintain all learners in the same remote room and allow them to complete the activity together virtually.

5. Help! I'm ready to give up!

Language Skill Focus	Listening and speaking with a writing extension
Language Functions Practiced	Giving advice, making suggestions, asking for clarification, expressing opinions
Grammar/Vocabulary Practiced	Modals, present tense, past tense, future tense, conditionals; vocabulary depends on content of the problems; use word banks to help students
Grouping Strategy	Individual, whole group
LAF Aspects	<ul><li>Personal and meaningful: learners are giving their own opinions and advice.</li><li>Engaging: learners stay actively involved because they must to complete the activity.</li><li>Interactive: learners interact with one another throughout the activity.</li><li>Cooperative: they must cooperate to complete the activity.</li><li>Repetition: there is repetition and restating constantly throughout the activity.</li><li>Higher order thinking: learners must think critically about how to help.</li><li>Purposeful: advice is being collected that can be useful.</li><li>Values diversity: a variety of perspectives and possibilities for completing the activity are possible.</li></ul>
Primary HoM Practiced	Persisting, Managing Impulsivity, Thinking Interdependently, Thinking Flexibly
Materials Needed	A set of problems that people need advice with. One is provided, but the teacher can create any set of problems and include vocabulary relevant to the class.

STEPS

- Give each learner one of the problems below, or create your own list of problems.
- If you have more than 15 students, you can have two groups going at once, or have learners pair up and share a problem.
- Have learners mingle, stating their problems and collecting advice from every other learner.
- To give lower level learners a scaffold, have them start their advice with the words, "Don't give up! You can (should, might, could, etc.)..." Model this several times.
- Learners write down the advice and the name of the person who gave it. Once they have collected advice from every other learner, they should put a star next to the best advice they received.
- At the end of the activity create a chart on the board with all learner names and put a tally mark next to the name of a learner every time he or she is chosen as having given the best advice. See who is the best advice giver in the class.

Sample problems to distribute:

I give up! I have a headache and nothing helps it go away!
I give up! I'm losing my hair and nothing I have tried works!
I give up! I can't find a boyfriend/girlfriend no matter what I do!
I give up! I can't stop hiccoughing no matter what I try!
I give up! My friend is mad at me no matter what I say!
I give up! There is a stain on my new sweater and I can't get it out!
I give up! My neighbor's dog won't stop barking! What can I do?
I give up! I have stage fright and need to perform!
I give up! I need to lose 10 pounds in two weeks or I won't fit into my wedding outfit!
I give up! I can't sleep at night. I'm losing my mind!
I give up! I need a raise or I can't pay my bills!
I give up! I'm scared of heights and I'm going mountain climbing!
I give up! I want to be rich but I can't save money!
I give up! I can't concentrate and I have a big test tomorrow!
I give up! I can't keep a secret and now everybody is mad at me!

Adaptations	Make it easier by doing this activity first as a whole group, giving modeling and scaffolds to learners in the form of sentence starters. Make it harder by offering complex problems that demand lengthier and more complicated advice.
Remote Learning	This activity can be done remotely by separating learners into small groups in remote learning rooms to gather advice from one another. Then bring them back into the main room to share what they have learned.

Chapter 7
LAF while Thinking Flexibly & Gathering Data Through all the Senses

The ability to think flexibly and the ability to gather data are among the most important thinking abilities. What is new and useful today can become outdated and irrelevant tomorrow. We can assume that technological advances and connection across languages and cultures will continue far into the foreseeable future, making the need to think flexibly and gather data in multiple ways even greater. As teachers, we need to prepare our language learners to be ready to meet the linguistic challenges of a changing world. One very important way to do this is to teach learners to think flexibly and gather data in multiple ways, so that when they encounter new problems and unforeseen situations, they can rise to the challenge of finding solutions, and they have the language skills they need to express those solutions.

Learners do not come with a set of instructions. Each of them is a unique individual that demands a unique teacher, even while that teacher has other equally unique learners. The same teaching activities that work for one group or individual may not work for all. Inevitably, we will fail if we do not think flexibly as educators. Our wonderful learners can be unpredictable and challenging, stubborn and unwilling to cooperate with our best teaching endeavors. We need to find ways to reach them when they are not responding the way we thought they would. We need to find ways to understand them when they confuse us, and we need to find ways to help them understand us. All of these multiple teaching skills demand flexible thinking and data gathering.

True Stories of TESOL

My experiences as a language teacher inside and outside of the classroom in Morocco taught me many things about being flexible and creative. One of the most important lessons I learned was that the concept of time varies across cultures. This came to light one day in Morocco when I attended a first birthday celebration. I had been living in Morocco for about nine months before the event, and I had already married into a Moroccan family. Although the family was wonderful and always very attentive to me, I still found it exhausting to spend a lot of time at Moroccan celebrations where I was not able to communicate effectively in Arabic.

On this day, I went with my husband to a birthday party for his one-year-old niece. The party started at approximately 10 in the morning and I was happy to be there. However, in my mind, a first birthday party that begins in the morning will undoubtedly be finished by mid-afternoon at the latest. That was my cultural expectation, and I was mentally prepared to remain at the party until at least three o'clock. I enjoyed playing with the baby and hanging out with my Moroccan family. I was surprised when the baby herself was not present at the party when we arrived. She came a few hours later with her grandparents, and stayed for only a short time. I found it curious, but not shocking. After all, every family and every culture has its own unique traditions and tendencies. I could adapt to that.

When lunch was served, I was put at the women's table. This was my first experience with gender separation at a party. I knew that this happened sometimes in Morocco, so I was not shocked. The worst thing about this for me was that the women spoke exclusively in Arabic at the women's table and my Arabic was extremely limited. For the two hours or so that the meal lasted, I was quiet. I smiled and nodded when it seemed appropriate. I tried not to feel paranoid when everyone was laughing and looking at me and I had no idea what they were saying. But it bothered me. After the meal, there was nothing happening (that I could determine) and I was ready to go home.

By then, it was already around four in the afternoon. I mentioned to my Moroccan husband that we should be leaving soon. He said we would leave soon. Two hours later I mentioned it again. He said we couldn't leave before eating *again*. The second meal came at some point, maybe around eight. Again, I was put at the women's table. Again, I had no way to participate in what looked to be a hilarious and engaging conversation. I started to get anxious. I wanted to go home. By this time it was around 10 in the evening. We had been at this first birthday for a full 12 hours. I excused myself from the women's table and approached my husband at the men's table, asking to speak to him in the kitchen. Everybody laughed.

I told my husband I had to leave. I could not stay any longer. He said we would leave when it was time to leave, and went back to the men's table. And that was when I lost it. I grabbed my purse, said goodbye, and headed out the door. It was not a good move. It caused quite a fracas that resulted in me hurrying down the sidewalk with my father-in-law and a long line of relatives following behind me, trying to stop me and talk to me. I felt humiliated, ridiculous, and like a petulant child.

I have thought back on this experience many times to try to understand what happened. I have come to the conclusion that I was most likely experiencing culture shock. I simply could not cope with being in what was essentially an all-Arabic environment for so many hours with virtually nobody trying to include me in conversations. It suddenly became overwhelming, and I had to escape. I have wondered why I couldn't just hang on, read a book, or simply sit there and smile, as was expected of me. I feel that I could do that now, but at the time I could not. Maybe the expectation I had in my head of what a first birthday party was, and the reality of what it actually was, became too much to cope with. Maybe the fact that I was put with all the women who mainly spoke Arabic, rather than the French I spoke with my husband, was too much for too long. I'm not sure, but after that experience I believed that I knew what culture shock feels like. It is when the new language and culture just become too much, too overwhelming, and there is a feeling of powerlessness in the situation. It is not pleasant.

I wish that all of those years ago in Morocco I could have been more flexible in my thinking. I wish I could have embraced the moment and laughed at myself for feeling paranoid or for my expectations of what a first birthday looks like. But I couldn't. I wish I could have enjoyed the sights, sounds, smells and flavors of that day, but I didn't. I hope that these experiences now help me to understand my students better and teach them about how valuable it is when we experience these moments to employ some of our Habits of Mind so we can get through them relatively unscathed.

Techniques for the Classroom: Visible Thinking

A great way to promote a culture of flexible thinking in the classroom is to take every opportunity to encourage learners to consider multiple perspectives when recounting an experience, or anticipating a new one. By implementing thinking routines into daily activities, parents and teachers can establish patterns of thinking that encourage learning throughout the day. A routine provides a pattern or process that is used repetitively to tackle complicated tasks, and to assist in the realization of goals. These routines can be used with any context and at virtually any time. As educators, we need to become aware and take advantage of every teachable moment. Establishing thinking routines as a regular interactive practice can help us to make the most of those often-unexpected opportunities.

Harvard's Project Zero has created and distributed visible thinking routines for use in classrooms that are easy to implement and extremely useful in fostering flexible thinking for learners. In addition, they provide an excellent source of activities that use language, are interactive and engaging, and meet the criteria of being language acquisition friendly (LAF) without being specifically designed for language learners. I have used many of these routines with language learners by providing small adaptations that act as linguistic scaffolds and supports. A great deal of information on these routines can be found online at the visiblethinking.org website, as well as many other websites devoted to disseminating this information. These routines are research based and very valuable in promoting thoughtful interaction among both children and adults. Some of the most useful visible thinking routines are listed below.

What Makes You Say That?

This routine encourages sharing multiple perspectives and opinions by having children view a picture, object or a situation, describe what they see happening using visible evidence, then interpret what they see. For language learners, it is especially important to model, use repetition, and to give sentence starters for them to express their ideas. This routine also provides a window into cultural perspectives of diverse learners.

See, Think, Wonder…

This routine also encourages thinking flexibly by having learners view a picture and first describe what they see, then express what they think about what they see, then be encouraged to explore what they 'wonder' about what they see. This next step in encouraging, 'wonder,' not only enhances flexible thinking; it also taps in to the Habit of Mind that focuses on creating, imagining and innovating. This is a great routine to use with learners of all ages. For language learners, the vocabulary that is offered in the 'see' part of the activity can be written on the board as a word bank, as can some of the full 'think' and 'wonder' sentences. Language learners may need more repetition and modeling than native speakers, and some scaffolding and prodding.

I used to think___, now I think___

This routine encourages all of us to reconsider opinions and beliefs we may have based on new evidence. It allows us to reexamine situations and consider them from different perspectives, to think flexibly and consider our own thinking. This type of thinking routine also automatically ties into the idea that we need to gather data with all the senses. Teachers can offer language learners many examples from their own lives. Examples that include how we need to change our thinking when we encounter a new language and culture are useful and something that our language learners can relate to.

There are many more visible thinking routines that have been created and established by Harvard's Project Zero (https://pz.harvard.edu/thinking-routines) and others. I encourage you to explore these online and to feel free to modify and adapt the thinking routines you discover to benefit your own teaching situations. Although each group of learners is unique, we all share many of the same issues and challenges and we can all benefit from thinking flexibly.

LAF in Class: Thinking Flexibly & Gathering Data Through all the Senses

1. Sunrise/Sunset

Language Skill Focus	Listening, speaking; reading and writing extensions possible
Language Functions Practiced	Justifying, describing, explaining, asking for clarification, expressing opinions
Grammar/Vocabulary Practiced	To like vs. to be like, adjectives, comparatives, present tense Vocabulary will include the categories chosen for the activity
Grouping Strategy	Whole group and half group, extension to individual and pair
LAF Aspects	<ul><li>Personal and meaningful: Learners are talking about themselves.</li><li>Engaging: Learners are actively involved throughout the activity through physical action and engaged interaction.</li><li>Interactive: Learners interact with one another throughout the activity.</li><li>Cooperative: Learners must cooperate to complete the activity.</li><li>Purposeful: Learners must choose a side and move to that area of the room.</li><li>Repetition: There is repetition and restating constantly throughout the half group portion of the activity.</li><li>Higher order thinking: Learners must think of critically about how to label themselves.</li><li>Values diversity: A variety of perspectives and possibilities for completing the activity are possible.</li></ul>
Primary HoM Practiced	Thinking Flexibly; Listening with Understanding and Empathy; Creating, Imagining and Innovating; Persisting; Thinking Interdependently; Gathering Data Through all the Senses
Materials Needed	None, but it is helpful to have a list of categories that you think will be fun for learners to grapple with before the start of the activity. Some potential categories are included below.

Sunrise/sunset is among my all-time favorite activities to do with language learners. I learned this as a cross-cultural training activity many years ago in Costa Rica and turned it into a LAF activity with some small modifications.

STEPS

- Write the following on the board: TO LIKE vs. TO BE LIKE.
- Ask learners to define each term and give synonyms and example sentences for each. I find that I always have some learners who understand the difference right away and can explain it, while others aren't sure.
- Offer the synonyms (if learners did not already do so) that *to like* is another way of saying to prefer something, and *to be like* is another way of saying to be similar to something.
- Ask learners if you can both 'like' and 'be like' something or someone. Solicit and/or give examples. Make sure they understand this is possible. For example, I like books, and my life story is like a book in that it has many chapters to it.
- Ask learners if you can 'be like' something you don't 'like.' Solicit and/or give examples. Make sure they understand this is possible: I don't like pigs but I can be very messy.
- Next, tell learners that in this activity you will give them two choices and they will chose which of the two they are *more like* (to be like=to be similar to), not which of the two they *like more* (to like=prefer).
- Tell learners to stand up and gather in the middle of the room.
- Use your hands to point to either side of the room. Learners must choose which word they are more like and go to that side of the room.
- One very important rule is that nobody can stay in the middle! They must pick a side. If you allow people to stay in the middle then everyone will stay in the middle because we are all multidimensional. The activity only works if learners pick a side.
- Demonstrate with the following choice: "Are you more like a sunrise, or a sunset?" Use your hands to direct everyone who is more like a sunrise to one side of the room, and those more like a sunset to the opposite side.
- Once learners have chosen a side, have them form a circle and take turns justifying or explaining their choice. Have them notice similarities and differences in explanations. If they are having a hard time with this give examples such as, "I am more like a sunset because I am calm and relaxed," or "I am more like a sunrise because I am bursting with energy," etc.
- Tell learners that there is no right answer, but they need to think flexibly and creatively to determine why they chose that side. If a learner says something like, "I prefer sunsets," remind them that it is not about what they LIKE more it is about what they are MORE LIKE.
- Go through at least five sets of choices, giving learners time in their side circles to justify and explain their choices before calling them all back to the middle for the next set of pairs.
- As an extension, ask learners to choose one of the things they felt they were more like and free write on that for a few minutes, then exchange papers with a peer and read and compare their ideas, then share with the whole class.

Below are some possible choices for this activity that demand that learners think creatively and flexibly. You can come up with your own ideas and include characters from readings, classroom objects, or vocabulary words you have been teaching.

sunrise	sunset
lion	kitten
circle	triangle
ocean	mountain
water	milk
pencil	pen
red	blue
plate	bowl
champagne	beer
bridge	tunnel

2. Amazing Art

Language Skill Focus	Listening and speaking
Language Functions Practiced	Describing, giving opinions, pondering, stating facts, questioning
Grammar/Vocabulary Practiced	Simple present, adjectives, nouns, conditionals Vocabulary depends on images but can include shapes, colors, objects and prepositions
Grouping Strategy	Individual, pair, whole group
LAF Aspects	3. Personal and meaningful: Learners are able to express their own ideas. 4. Engaging: Learners are actively engaged throughout the activity. 5. Uses visuals: Visuals are essential to this activity. 6. Interactive: Learners interact with one another as well as with the teacher. 7. Cooperative: They must cooperate to complete the activity. 8. Repetition: There is natural repetition and restating as they participate. 9. Higher order thinking: Thinking continues to increase in level as the activity progresses to the wonder stage. 10. Values diversity: All opinions and ideas are welcome.
Primary HoM Practiced	Thinking Flexibly, Thinking Interdependently, Creating, Imagining and Innovating
Materials Needed	Actual or virtual works of art, newsprint, paper or a board of some kind to write on, markers or pens

For this activity, we use the visible thinking strategy, 'See, Think, Wonder.'

STEPS

- First, do an Internet search for images of 'amazing' works of art. This will vary depending on what you and your learners consider 'amazing.' You can also use art books or actual paintings or drawings if you have those available. I like to use well-known masterpieces as well as modern art, primitive art, children's book illustrations, and lesser known artists for this activity so that we end up with a great mix of styles, content and perspectives. Another option is to ask your language learners to share art they love from their home cultures or other.

- Give your learners a few minutes to simply 'see' the art, and then ask them: "What do you see?"

- Encourage as many details as possible and write these down on newsprint, a whiteboard or whatever you have handy.

- Option: create a semantic web with this by putting the word 'see' in the middle of a circle (or an eyeball) and writing in spokes around it, creating categories as they come up.

- Another option is to make a chart with three columns labeled, 'see, think, and wonder,' or create whatever graphic organizer you wish to create, or have none at all. I have drawn a giant eye for 'see' and written inside of it, a brain for 'think,' and a cloud bubble coming out of a head for 'wonder.' Do whatever feels natural for you.

- After you have covered just about everything that can literally be seen in the artwork, ask: "What do you think about that?" or "What do you think about when you see this?"

- Again, jot down the contributions of your learners, ask follow up questions as you think of them and encourage learners to listen to one another. You should find that they build off of one another's ideas, thus expanding language practice and connecting.

- Finally, ask: "What does it make you wonder?" Model a response if learners are unsure of what to say.

- Encourage language learners to be as creative and imaginative as they want to be, and do not judge responses, just write down key words and ideas offered. You should find that as the thinking becomes more abstract, the language your learners produce also becomes more abstract, longer, more complex and more infused with meaning and significance.

This activity is a great thinking routine that leads to many expansion activities. For example, learners can create stories or dialogues related to the art. They can do readings or write about the art, or role play interviewing the artist. The only limit to this activity is the imagination of you and your language learners. In other words, it is limitless.

Adaptations	<u>Make it easier</u>: Give learners examples and modeling before asking them to contribute their own ideas. You may use an image that they are familiar with from a classroom resource or that includes many things that you have already taught them in terms of vocabulary. You might have a pre-made word bank that they can pull from. <u>Make it harder</u>: Use images that are more complex and busy. Give less modeling and prompting and encourage learners to build off of one another's responses.
Remote Learning	This activity is easily adapted to remote learning. You can display an image and go about the same steps you would in a face-to-face classroom, with students contributing their ideas one at a time. It is helpful to build a word bank as you proceed with the activity for lower level learners.

3. What Would You Do?

Language Skill Focus	Listening and speaking
Language Functions Practiced	Describing, giving opinions, pondering, suggesting
Grammar/Vocabulary Practiced	Modals, conditionals Vocabulary: depends on materials used
Grouping Strategy	Individual, small group, whole group
LAF Aspects	• Personal and meaningful: Learners are talking about their own ideas. • Engaging: Learners are thinking about and giving opinions on controversial topics. • Uses visuals: Videos and illustrations can be used. • Interactive: Learners interact with one another to complete the task. • Cooperative: Learners cooperate in small groups to complete the activity. • Repetition: There is repetition and restating as they describe their ideas. • Higher order thinking: Learners have to come up with ideas about what they would do in given circumstances that have no easy answer. • Values diversity: Different ways of seeing the world and behaving are part of the activity.
Primary HoM Practiced	Thinking Flexibly, Thinking Interdependently, Gathering Data Through all the Senses

Materials Needed	Videos or readings from books, plays or short stories that feature a character that has to make a difficult choice. These can be found online or in the library. Many children's picture books involve characters having to make difficult choices. Picture books are excellent tools for the language learning classroom no matter the age of the participants. They are brief, illustrated (with illustrations often telling half or more of the story), windows into the target language and culture, and generally enjoyable. Another possibility for this activity is to use short video clips from the program of the same name, "What Would You Do?" (found on YouTube), or clips about difficult choices from many movies such as *Stand By Me* and *Sophie's Choice*. If you are going to use videos with language learners be sure to keep the clips very short. Research indicates that you shouldn't go beyond a few minutes for language education purposes or language learners will often tune out and lose the thread of the video.

STEPS

- Start off by reading or watching together as a class the material you have chosen that features one or more characters needing to make a controversial or difficult choice.
- Once the material has been read or viewed (with comprehension checks and scaffolding as needed), conduct a brief question/answer session with your learners to recall the choice that was made and ascertain that everyone understood the story.
- Brainstorm other choices that the character might have made as a whole group.
- Write ideas on a board or on a paper so that key words and information are reviewed and remembered.
- Have learners work in pairs or small cooperative groups to rewrite the scene as if they were the main characters and were responsible for the choices made and the consequences of those choices.
- Remind learners that "What would you do?" is the primary question asked, and there is no one predetermined correct answer, but rather a variety of possibilities in any scenario. Many choices can be influenced by cultural background and most choices can involve both positive and negative consequences.
- Encourage your learners to put themselves in the shoes of the character, creating empathy and understanding, and then use the information they have to make a different choice.
- Another variation is to present the literature or the video but not let the learners see what choice was ultimately made, and have them create the scenario that predicts the choices.
- Present new choices to the class through role playing activities, discussion or in a written format, depending on what language skills you would like to practice most. I find that role plays are usually successful and enjoyable ways for learners to present their ideas, and these can later be journaled about to extend the language practice.

Adaptations	<u>Make it easier:</u> Give learners scenarios, videos or readings that are short and easy to understand. Use picture books for extra context or short video clips from television shows or movies they are familiar with. <u>Make it harder:</u> Give learners longer prompts from videos or books to consider. Ask them to come up with their own difficult choices from their personal lives or other areas. Give less modeling and scaffolding.
Remote Learning	This activity is easily adapted to remote learning. You can give the short reading or video to learners before the class and go over it during class, encouraging learners to give their opinions. You can then separate learners into small groups with a new prompt or the same prompt to develop short role plays, then have them rejoin the group to demonstrate what they have done. Learners may also create their own videos or scenarios to share with one another.

4. Mind-bending Math

Language Skill Focus	Listening, speaking
Language Functions Practiced	Describing, giving opinions, pondering, giving and following directions
Grammar/Vocabulary Practiced	Simple present, comparatives Vocabulary: words for size, shape, and location
Grouping Strategy	Individual, pairs
LAF Aspects	<ul><li>Personal and meaningful: Learners are creating their own problems.</li><li>Engaging: They are doing something that is hands on while learning language so they are engaged physically.</li><li>Uses visuals: The building blocks themselves are the visuals.</li><li>Interactive: Learners interact with one another to complete the task.</li><li>Cooperative: They must cooperate in pairs to complete the activity.</li><li>Repetition: There is repetition and restating as they describe.</li><li>Higher order thinking: Learners have to come up with problems rather than simply repeating information.</li><li>Values diversity: Different ways of stating math problems and thinking about math are valued and encouraged.</li></ul>
Primary HoM Practiced	Thinking Flexibly, Gathering Data Through all the Senses, Thinking Interdependently, Creating, Imagining and Innovating
Materials Needed	Blocks, Legos, unit cubes, beans, pasta or any other thing that is countable and can be manipulated and grouped. Newsprint or a board to write on and any writing implement.

For this activity, language learners will be working with math concepts and visual/spatial principles. Although your focus is on teaching language and giving language practice, it is often a good idea to integrate a task that takes the focus off of language so that using the language as a tool to complete the task generates the possibility of extended and natural language practice. Many times students will 'forget' that they are using the language because they are so involved in resolving the task. This is ideal for developing fluency and turning off the 'monitor' (Krashen, 1982) that makes our learners worry that they might be making mistakes and hesitant to use language.

STEPS

- Gather your countable materials and put them in a pile in the center of a table or on the floor in the center of a circle you create. Start out by having learners count the number of objects present.
- Ask learners what they think you will be doing with the objects. Encourage all kinds of ideas, and actually do some of them if they are reasonable math activities that are enjoyable and encourage language practice.
- Next, separate the learners into pairs and give them a random amount of objects.
- Ask learner pairs to take turns creating as many different kinds of math problems as they can with the objects they have, and to write out these problems using only words.
- Next, learner pairs pass word problems around for other pairs to solve.
- For a variation, have learners create math problems with the manipulatives that their partners are not allowed to see. They must only feel the question and answer with their hands, or that they can only 'listen' to (such as by dropping objects one by one, etc.). This should encourage gathering data through multiple senses and encourage some thinking out loud.

Adaptations	<u>Make it easier</u>: Do the activity as a whole class first, modeling problems that you create for your students. Allow students many opportunities to see the activity in action and create a semantic map on the board with different problem possibilities and vocabulary that goes with each. <u>Make it harder</u>: Do less modeling with students at the beginning of the activity and give students more objects to work with. Giving students a very limited amount of time also helps to make the activity more challenging.
Remote Learning	This is a difficult one to do remotely because the students will not have access to the materials in the same location. However, it can be done with some adaptation by asking students to collect a number of objects they can use as manipulatives at home. This could be pieces of macaroni pasta, paper clips or other things that they might have in abundance. They would then need to send one another photographs or show their problems through a webcam to their partners.

5. Agree/Disagree Circle

Language Skill Focus	Listening, speaking
Language Functions Practiced	Agreeing, disagreeing, giving opinions, pondering, commenting
Grammar/Vocabulary Practiced	Simple present, conditionals, modals Vocabulary: words depend on topics chosen for the activity
Grouping Strategy	Individual, whole group
LAF Aspects	• Personal and meaningful: Learners are expressing their own ideas. • Engaging: Learners are actively engaged in listening throughout the activity. • Interactive: Learners interact with one another to complete the task. • Cooperative: Learners must cooperate to complete the task as they cannot repeat one another. • Repetition: There is natural repetition of sentence starters and forms as the activity progresses around the circle. • Higher order thinking: Learners have to come up with new and creative ways to agree and disagree with the prompt. • Values diversity: Different ways of thinking are valued and encouraged.
Primary HoM Practiced	Thinking Flexibly, Thinking Interdependently, Creating, Imagining and Innovating, Communicating with Clarity and Precision
Materials Needed	None are necessary but it is a good idea to have pre-prepared sentences to work from to start the activity. These can be created based on topics the class is learning about or any somewhat controversial topic.

STEPS

- For this thinking game, join learners in a large circle. It is best when there are no more than 15 in the circle.
- Make a statement that offers an opinion on some topic that is relevant to your learners. These topics will depend on age, context, and language level. Example sentences are included below.
- Explain to students that you will be going around the circle three times. The first time around, going clockwise, everyone needs to agree with your sentence. The second time around, going in the opposite direction, everyone needs to disagree with the same sentence. The third time around, going again in the clockwise direction, everyone needs to offer a comment that neither agrees nor disagrees with the initial sentence.
- Start by stating your sentence. We will use the example, "Everyone should learn to swim."
- Go around the circle once *clockwise*, with each student creating a sentence that is in agreement with the initial sentence, for example, "I agree, everyone should learn to swim because swimming is good exercise."
- Important note: no repeats! Learners have to listen and come up with a new reason to agree.
- After everyone has spoken, go *counter-clockwise* around the circle with every learner disagreeing with the initial sentence. For example, "I disagree, not everyone needs to learn to swim because not everyone lives near water."
- Finally, go around the circle a third time with each student giving a related sentence that is neither in agreement or in disagreement with the original sentence: "If everyone learns to swim, then more people will buy swimsuits."
- Remember, no repeats!
- Let students have one 'pass' per game. If they just can't think of anything to say on one round, they can 'pass,' but only once in the three times around the circle.
- This game forces students to listen and think flexibly.

Possible Sentences to Use:

Everyone should get married.
All kids should have a pet.
Teachers should get paid more than principals.
All men should grow beards.
All houses should be painted white.
Shoes should not be worn indoors.
Parents should choose careers for their kids.
Everyone should learn to swim.
Nobody should have plastic surgery.
All teenagers should travel internationally.
Cars should be outlawed.

Adaptations	<u>Make it easier</u>: Use sentences that have many possible reasons for someone to agree or disagree. Model several examples and give learners hints if they get stuck. <u>Make it harder</u>: Do less modeling with learners at the beginning of the activity and give students more challenging sentences to work with.
Remote Learning	This is a difficult one to do remotely, but it can be done by putting learners in a virtual circle and calling out each learner's name when it is his or her turn.

Chapter 8
LAF while Finding Humor & Taking Responsible Risks

What can be easier than finding humor in our daily lives as language learners and language teachers? The voyage into new languages and cultures is ripe with opportunities for humor. At the same time, sometimes it is tough to find humor in situations that are difficult or trying as we go about the enormous responsibilities we face as the guides and teachers of our learners. Nevertheless, it is those challenging times when finding humor becomes most necessary, because humor will help us navigate through them. When we are able to traverse difficult situations in the classroom with humor, we serve as positive role models for our learners. A smile, a joke, and a teacher with a lighthearted manner shows learners that finding humor is a helpful way to deal with the failures and disappointments that are an inescapable and important aspect of our daily lives.

True stories from the world of TESOL

In order to connect with my teacher education students and language learners, I often tell them anecdotes about my own experiences as a language learner and a cross cultural trainer in the U.S. and abroad. My stories often revolve around my experiences as a language teacher in Morocco. When I first arrived in Morocco and began to work at the American Language Center in Casablanca, I was introduced to a number of the teachers already working there. Many of these teachers were missionaries from the United States who had gone to Morocco to teach Christian principles to Muslims. They apparently were not paid very well and also had to secure teaching jobs in order to make a living. I was one of the few teachers at the language center at that time who had a degree in TESOL, teaching experience, and cross-cultural training abroad.

Because of my experience, and despite my youth, I was asked to provide some training for the older teachers who had already been there for a while. Their teaching success was limited, and the director of the language center thought that I might be able to help. Unfortunately, older teachers often resent being trained by younger teachers and I received a bit of push back, but in general the training went well. At the end of the training one of the older teachers who was an American missionary said to me, "Thanks, and welcome to Morocco where the normal is bizarre and the bizarre is normal." At first I didn't understand what he meant and I thought he was probably not very culturally sensitive, but soon I got the idea. In Morocco, what seemed 'normal' behavior to me in many situations was absolutely taboo or just plain strange, and what seemed 'bizarre' behavior to me was perfectly acceptable and normal there. I probably have scores of anecdotes that highlight this difference but I will tell a linguistic one here that required me to find humor very quickly.

Soon after arriving in Morocco to teach English, I unexpectedly and without much careful deliberation married a charming Moroccan man who did not speak English or Spanish, the two languages I spoke at the time. He spoke three languages, as do many Moroccans: classical Arabic, Moroccan Arabic, and French. All I can say is that I was young and impulsive and in love. Unsurprisingly, we are no longer married. Nevertheless we were married for a number of years and those first few years we lived in Morocco. Thus, I became part of a Moroccan family after being in the country a very short amount of time.

In this particular family, only the younger generation spoke French. Therefore, in order to communicate with my in-laws and grandmother in-law I needed to learn some Arabic quickly. By the time I married my husband, only a few months into living in Morocco, I already spoke a good amount of French. I apparently had French somewhere in my brain left over from early childhood and I found it easy to pick up, but that's another story.

I have always loved to learn about other cultures and languages and I quickly started to try to learn as much Moroccan Arabic as possible. One day I was taught what to say when somebody sneezes, a kind of 'bless you' comment that is appropriate in Moroccan Arabic. I will not even dare to try to spell it out phonetically here. You will soon see why.

My new husband and I went to his parents' home every Saturday for 'lunch.' I put quotations around the word because these lunches lasted considerably longer than any lunch I have ever experienced in my life before or since. We would get to his parents' home around noon and the lunch experience would not be over until at least 8 p.m. For me this was exhausting, as I was immersed for hours in a virtually Arabic-only environment. My new husband usually spent most of his time hanging out with his pals in the neighborhood (all men--women didn't hang with the men outside) and left me with his mother, his aunt and sometimes his elderly grandmother. All three of these women were wonderful, loving, and bent over backwards to please me with their faces and gestures, but there was hardly a word that passed between us.

In my Moroccan family the grandmother, who we called M'Aziza, was highly respected and revered. She was very old school, sitting only on the carpet, never on a sofa or a chair. She had the tattoos on her forehead and around her wrists and ankles that spoke of women from a bygone era. Everyone loved her very much, and I learned to kiss her palm as did her grandchildren and children whenever entering a room where she sat.

On one of our extremely long lunch experiences my husband and his siblings had remained with me and we were chatting away in French. They would also go back and forth in Arabic with their parents and grandmother but for me there was always a translation. I suppose that I was feeling pretty happy, relaxed and a part of the family by then because I decided to try out my Arabic at a crucial moment that will live in infamy.

M'Aziza apparently had a cold and let out a soft sneeze. I immediately responded to her sneeze with my version of 'bless you' in Moroccan Arabic, putting to use a word I had recently learned. What happened next will never be erased from my memory. My husband and his sister both literally got up from where they were seated and starting rolling on the floor laughing. I had never previously seen anyone literally roll on the floor laughing, but there they were. I sat watching them in horror. M'Aziza did not crack a smile or make any comment, she just sat there like a statue observing her grandchildren's shenanigans. Every time my husband was able to take a breath, he would look at me, start to talk, then burst back into hysterical laughter. I was mortified. Eventually, and it took a while, it was explained to me that I had evidently laid a pretty horrible insult on their grandmother. Apparently the expression for 'bless you' I had been taught and the word for this insult are practically identical (to my ear) and I had said one instead of the other. That was literally the last time I ever tried to say 'bless you' in Morocco, and also the last time I attempted to speak Arabic for a while.

Obviously, this experience put a damper on my Arabic language learning. I felt humiliated and stupid and didn't even want to try to speak. However, and luckily, I soon got over it and was able to see the humor in the situation. Nobody was angry with me, they just found it hilarious. I decided to be happy that I had given them a good laugh and to use this anecdote with my language learners to show them that we all make mistakes with pronunciation, and it is okay.

The use of humor in that situation (as opposed to shame) truly helped me to embrace my role as a new member of a Moroccan family and my role as a language and culture learner. I often use humor with my learners. I find that when we can turn a language gaffe into something to laugh about, we are able to get more done linguistically, better navigate new cultures, and enjoy the process of learning even more.

Humor in the classroom

A good sense of humor is one of the characteristics associated with a general sense of well-being and success (Seligman, 2002). This is essential to the language classroom. If a learner does not feel comfortable and successful, it is very difficult to learn language. Developing a good sense of humor may not be something that we have traditionally thought of as an important part of language acquisition, yet maybe we should. Considering the importance of humor in improving our physical health (laughter strengthens muscles and releases endorphins in the bloodstream) and personal satisfaction, as well as increasing our ability to manage stress, anxiety and even grief, being able to find humor seems to be an important skill that should be encouraged and practiced both inside and outside of the classroom.

If we examine the media that we seek out for pleasure, it is easy to see the importance of humor in our lives. A great deal of what we engage with is designed to entertain us by making us laugh. The pursuit of laughter influences many of our decisions on a daily basis. It plays an essential role in deciding what movies we watch, books we read, websites we visit, television we consume, advertisements we remember, events we participate in, and friends we interact with. Although it is not the only factor that we consider when choosing our activities, it certainly does have a profound influence on how we structure our free time.

At the same time, failed attempts at humor can be very destructive to social and cross-cultural relationships and can be a barrier to learning. For example, teasing, and joking at inappropriate times, or without the implicit understanding of both parties that it is a joke, can easily backfire. Language learners who feel as though they are being laughed at or ridiculed are understandably reluctant to take risks in the target language by interacting with others. Because interaction is essential to language acquisition, and because the comfort of our learners and their feeling of being safe in our classrooms is of primary importance, it is necessary that we be cautious with our use of humor as teachers. We need to model for all learners when empathy is needed instead of laughter. By integrating humor within our teaching we practice understanding others and ourselves while maintaining a light and uplifting learning environment, but we must be culturally sensitive and aware of how we are using humor at all times.

Techniques for the classroom

In order to make sure that I incorporate a healthy dose of humor in my teaching every day, I try to remember the acronym LAUGH and weave it in to my teaching and learning activities. I also teach this acronym to my language learners.

L – Listen to those around you when you are out in public. You can often hear a funny story or situation merely by eavesdropping. Tell these stories to your students and encourage them to do the same. Retelling funny everyday events or unexpected things that happen to you is one way to practice language. It also acts as a window into the target culture. We can learn a lot about a culture by understanding what is funny to native speakers.

A – Act silly whenever you get a chance, and whenever the situation is demanding a lightening of the mood. It is a great teaching tool to be silly sometimes, and it gets the attention of students right away. Using body language as part of your teacher communication tools is essential to providing comprehensible input for language learners. Sometimes I feel silly with my exaggerated facial gestures and body movements when trying to explain a word or situation, and students often laugh at my antics. However, I can take being laughed at a little bit if it helps my students understand what I am trying to say and helps them retain the information.

U – Use your own faults, failures, and foibles as a source of laughter. I find that my students always appreciate and get a good laugh out of the errors and gaffes I have made as a language learner. They very much enjoy correcting me and teaching me things about their own languages and cultures. They also learn to laugh at themselves when they make mistakes.

G – Gather a couple of jokes you can tell well. If you can, make it a habit to memorize funny jokes that you hear or read and retell them. If you are not a joke person, maybe you can use puns or riddles instead. You never know when a good joke, pun, or riddle will come in handy, and it can serve to create connections between you and your language learners. Sharing a good laugh is always a helpful and bonding experience. With my language learners, I like to tell jokes and puns that revolve around language and culture issues. I also encourage them to tell me jokes in English that come from their own languages and cultures. Sometimes we find that jokes simply do not translate, and other times they do. This is a nice way to open classes and encourage interaction.

H – Help others to see the humor in difficult situations. Sometimes language learners take their learning process too seriously and become highly discouraged if they don't feel that they are making progress quickly enough. Help your learners see that a language error today is often funny a week later. Remind them that they are on a language learning journey that will have many ups and downs and that learning to laugh at themselves is one way to make the journey more enjoyable.

LAF in Class: Finding Humor & Taking Responsible Risks

1. Comic Conversations

Language Skill Focus	Reading, writing
Language Functions Practiced	Asking and answering questions, giving information
Grammar/Vocabulary Practiced	Interrogatives, modals, simple present, present continuous, simple past Vocabulary depends on comic topics but could include question words, adjectives, adverbs and exclamations
Grouping Strategy	Individual, pairs
LAF Aspects	<ul><li>Personal and meaningful: Learners are creating something of their own.</li><li>Engaging: Learners are actively engaged in their comic creation.</li><li>Uses visuals: Learners create their own visuals.</li><li>Interactive: Learners interact with one another to complete the task.</li><li>Cooperative. Learners cooperate in pairs to complete the activity.</li><li>Repetition: There is repetition and restating as they decide on their comic strip.</li><li>Higher order thinking: Learners have to come up with a their own narrative to match pictures.</li><li>Values diversity: Different ways of seeing the world are inherent in the activity.</li></ul>
Primary HoM Practiced	Finding Humor, Thinking Flexibly, Thinking Interdependently, Taking Responsible Risks, Creating, Imagining and Innovating, Communicating with Clarity and Precision
Materials Needed	Either real or teacher-created comic strips with between one and three illustrations with the speech bubbles blanked out.

STEPS

- Start by showing several simple comic strips from newspapers that you think your learners will find funny. "Peanuts" is a good comic strip to use for this as the jokes are generally easily understood.
- Show another comic strip where you have blanked out the speech bubbles and ask the class to work together in pairs or small groups to come up with what might be said in each bubble based on the drawings.
- Encourage sharing of ideas and write key words on the board.
- Reveal the actual words that were in the speech bubbles and see if anyone came up with the same words or something close to them. Explain the humor if necessary.
- Have students pair up.
- Distribute comic strips of one to three squares with speech bubbles blanked out.
- Have pairs work together to fill in the bubbles, creating their own comics based on the drawings.

An advantage of this activity for language learners is that it allows them to be creative in the target language while demanding a very small number of words and giving visual context. As a follow up, you can have learners work to create their own short comic strip from scratch based on something funny that happened to them in their own lives or based solely on their imaginations.

Adaptations	Make it easier: Give learners more comics to look at and modeling of filling in blanks as a group before you begin. Keep a word/phrase bank on the board with expressions they might want to use.
	Make it harder: Give comics with more panels that are more complicated to fill in. Encourage learners to make their own comics once the initial activity is over.
Remote Learning	This activity can be adapted to remote learning by providing the blanked out comics to learners in pairs and separating them from the whole group to work together in remote rooms, then coming back to present to the whole group.

2. Picture Stories

Language Skill Focus	Reading, writing
Language Functions Practiced	Making assumptions, predicting, elaborating, concluding
Grammar/Vocabulary Practiced	Modals, simple present, present continuous, simple past, future tense Vocabulary depends on what is depicted in each picture received.
Grouping Strategy	Individual, small group
LAF Aspects	<ul><li>Personal and meaningful: Learners are creating their own story so it is personal.</li><li>Engaging: Learners are actively engaged in their story creations throughout the activity.</li><li>Uses visuals: Pictures are provided.</li><li>Interactive: Learners interact with one another through writing to complete the task.</li><li>Cooperative: Learners cooperate in small groups to complete the activity.</li><li>Repetition: There is repetition and restating as they decide on their final story.</li><li>Higher order thinking: Learners have to come up with a their own narrative to match pictures while using transitions from one learner to the next to keep the flow of the story going.</li><li>Values diversity: Different ways of seeing the world are inherent in the activity; perceptions of each learner are part of the narrative.</li></ul>
Primary HoM Practiced	Finding Humor; Taking Responsible Risk; Thinking Flexibly; Thinking Interdependently; Creating, Imagining and Innovating; Communicating with Clarity and Precision
Materials Needed	Pictures that seem to tell a story cut out of magazines, lined paper and a writing instrument for each learner. The activity works best when the pictures are interesting and each person writes with a different color. Mount pictures on card stock or folders to keep them usable over time. Use a timer if you have one.

STEPS

This activity is best done in groups of four, however it can be adapted to bigger groups or reduced to a small group of three participants.

- Arrange learners in a small circle or square facing away from one another so that they cannot see the paper in front of their partners.
- Each learner is given one picture and one piece of lined paper and a pen or a pencil.
- Tell each participant that they will have three minutes to look at their picture and begin to write a story about the picture.
- Emphasize to learners that they will not be describing the picture, but rather writing the beginning of the story. Model this with a picture you have not distributed.
- Encourage learners to use their imaginations as they begin to write the story of their pictures.
- Set up a timer so that after three minutes, everyone puts down the pen they are using, **even if they are in the middle of a sentence** and passes both their paper and their picture clockwise.
- During this part of the activity, give learners a few minutes to read what the first learner who received the picture wrote, and to look carefully at the picture given.
- The learner then *continues* writing the story that the first learner started. Emphasize that they will not be starting a whole new story, they need to continue the story started by the other learner. Thus each learner in this round imagines and writes how the story would continue that was started by the person that passed the paper and picture to him or her.
- After five minutes or so, the timer goes off again and the cycle is repeated with the third person continuing the story built by the first two.
- Finally, on the last round, the last person (when it is a group of 4) concludes the story by reading what the previous three participants wrote as beginning, first middle, then second middle.
- Once each learner has started, built on, and concluded four stories from four pictures, everyone in the cooperative group turns around their chairs to face one another.
- During the activity, especially during the last two turns, plenty of giggling and laughing is usually heard as learners read how stories have been evolving and add their own humor. Although this activity is not meant specifically to create humorous stories, I find that most of the stories end up being humorous no matter what pictures are used as prompts.
- To finish off the activity, have learner cooperative groups read all of the stories they have created out loud to one another, then choose the one they like best.
- Learners can add a title and any edits they want to add to their chosen story.
- Finally, learners 'publish' their final, cooperatively created story by putting it up on a wall next to the picture and sharing it with the whole class.

Adaptations	<u>Make it Easier:</u> This activity can be simplified by giving learners sentence stems to start them off with and by modeling how it is to be done several times. There can also be a word bank on the board that corresponds to the images so that learners can pick vocabulary that is appropriate. <u>Make it harder:</u> This activity can be made more challenging by making sure that the pictures provided are complex and open to a number of interpretations. Cutting down on the time that everyone has to write also adds to the difficulty.
Remote Learning	This particular activity is more difficult to adapt to remote learning since the learners cannot sit in a back-to-back formation and pass the pictures to one another. When done in a real classroom, plenty of laughter and giggling can be heard as learners read one another's comments and this adds to the engagement of the activity. One way to adapt this might be to provide each learner in the class with an image and give them 3 minutes to write the beginning of the story based on that image, then have each learner pass their beginning and the image to a chosen student, continuing by passing to another etc. Then the four students who worked on the same pictures would get together in a break out room and continue with the activity. This would take a lot of planning and logistics to make sure that the stories are passed in a way that allows all learners to write introductions, continuing narratives and conclusions.

3. Confessions and Challenges

Language Skill Focus	Reading, speaking
Language Functions Practiced	Explaining, surmising, making predictions, giving opinions
Grammar/Vocabulary Practiced	Modals, simple present, present continuous, simple past, future tense Vocabulary depends on confession and challenges cards; vocabulary should be familiar to students or slightly more than what they know.
Grouping Strategy	Individual, small group
LAF Aspects	• Personal and meaningful: Learners are talking about themselves. • Engaging: Learners are actively engaged as listeners and speakers. • Uses visuals: Pictures can be provided. • Interactive: Learners interact with one another to complete the task. • Cooperative: Learners cooperate in small groups to complete the activity. • Repetition: There is repetition and restating as they give their opinions and explanations. • Higher order thinking: Learners have to come up with their own responses to challenging questions. • Values diversity: Different ways of seeing the world are inherent in the activity; ways of knowing of each learner dictate the interactions.
Primary HoM Practiced	Finding Humor; Taking Responsible Risks; Thinking Flexibly; Thinking Interdependently; Creating, Imagining & Innovating; Communicating with Clarity & Precision
Materials Needed	Pre-prepared 'confessions' and 'challenges' cards (and for dramatic effect, a high stool and a microphone or a fake microphone on a stand for those learners who are artistically or dramatically inclined).

STEPS

- Write the English language expression, "Comedy is tragedy plus time," and ask your language learners what they think this mean. Welcome all ideas.
- If your learners have not already come up with the meaning, explain to them that the meaning of the expression can be applied to each of us by thinking about it in our own lives. When we look back to situations that we have faced in the past, we can often laugh at ourselves and turn those tragedies into funny anecdotes that allow us to connect with others.
- Solicit examples of this from your language learners and model by providing an anecdote of your own.
- Ask your learners if they have example expressions in their native languages with a similar meaning that they can share with the whole class. By asking learners about their own first language and cultural knowledge you are creating an environment that values diversity and being a culturally responsive teacher.
- Have language learners take turns picking cards out of a hat or any other object (such as a bowl or a bag) and follow the directions on the card. The cards are either 'confessions' or 'challenges.'
- I find it works better not to allow learners to pick from clearly marked piles of confessions or challenges, but rather to randomly get what they get, thereby increasing a little bit the 'risky' nature of the activity and the need to use creative and critical thinking skills.
- For the confessions cards, the learners are asked to 'confess' to one of the prompts. For the challenges cards they are asked to do something that is a bit risky or challenging and can also be funny.
- Five 'confessions' and five 'challenges' cards are offered below as examples. These can be easily adapted for different groups of learners. As the teacher, you know your learners best and will be able to develop cards that will best lead to engaged language practice for your particular group.

Confessions Cards:

Tell us about an embarrassing experience you had that you find funny now.	Tell about a time you lied when you were younger that seems funny now when you look back on it.
Tell us something you loved to do when you were younger that seems strange or funny now.	Tell us about how your pet or your favorite thing (such as your car, a book, or other) would complain about you if they could.
Tell us about a prank or joke you once pulled or that you would pull again if you could (the word 'prank' may need to be explained).	Tell us about a time you pretended to like something or someone you didn't like.

Challenges Cards:

Tell a joke, riddle or a pun. Make one up or repeat one you know that you think is funny.	Bark, meow, or growl the tune to a famous song so we can guess what it is.
Describe a well-known television show or current event as if you were a famous historical character or cartoon figure so we can guess who it is.	Act out a math problem using only body language but not your hands so we can guess what it is.
Do a quick sketch of your favorite song, book or movie so we can guess what it is.	If you had to be an animal, which animal would you be and why?

Adaptations	<u>Make it easier</u> by creating cards that have simpler tasks written in simpler language and giving more modeling and examples. You can also have learners do this in pairs to lower the affective filter and increase the likelihood that learners will take risks. <u>Make it harder</u> by creating cards that have more complicated and demanding tasks that require greater language use. You can also have learners create cards for the game for writing practice and to make it more student directed.
Remote Learning	This activity can easily be adapted to remote learning by creating a numbered list of mixed confessions and challenges instead of cards. Learners should not see the list. Have each learner pick a number when it is her turn, then show the confession or challenge on your screen so everyone can see it. Make sure not to show the whole list so learners cannot pick something they want but rather have the challenge of having to talk about whatever they randomly choose.

4. Rethinking Mother Goose

Focus On	Speaking, listening
Language Functions	Agreeing, disagreeing, giving opinions, contradicting, supporting
Grammar/ Vocabulary Practice	Declaratives Vocabulary will depend on the content of the nursery rhymes chosen.
LAF Aspects	• Personal and meaningful: Learners are reimagining something according to their personal experiences and choices. • Engaging: Learners are actively engaged as listeners, speakers and creators. • Uses visuals: Pictures can be provided to go with the rhymes. • Interactive: Learners interact with one another to complete the task. • Cooperative: Learners cooperate in pairs or small groups to complete the activity. • Repetition: There is repetition as rhymes are taught and then repeated for intonation and rhythm. • Higher order thinking: Learners have to come up with a reimagined rhyme. • Values diversity: Different ways of seeing the world are inherent in the activity.
Primary HoM Practiced	Finding Humor; Creating, Imagining and Innovating; Taking Responsible Risks; Communicating with Clarity and Precision
Materials	Several classic English language nursery rhymes that can be found on the internet, such as *Jack & Jill, Little Bo Peep, Humpty Dumpty, Hey Diddle, Diddle, Mary Had a Little Lamb* and many more. Category cards with topics like FOOD, HEALTH, SPORTS, ENTERTAINMENT, TRAVEL, WORK, MUSIC, WEATHER, etc.

STEPS

- Gather several classic nursery rhymes to work with. These can be found free online or in books.
- Read a short and simple one out loud to learners, allowing them to see the words as you read. If you have visuals that go along with the nursery rhyme, that is even better.
- Answer any questions learners might have about the rhyme, and do several choral readings of the rhyme with learners. Point out how the intonation, pronunciation, and rhythm of the rhyme feels.
- Pick a category out of a hat or a box. Ask learners how they might reimagine the nursery rhyme using that topic as a focus. For example reimagine *Jack & Jill* with a focus on FOOD.
- Brainstorm with learners to see what they come up with. Help them along.

For example, using the rhyme Jack and Jill:

Jack and Jill went up a hill
To fetch a pail of water.
Jack fell down and broke his crown,
And Jill came tumbling after.

Using the category FOOD, this rhyme could turn into:

Jack and Jill went to a restaurant
To eat a lovely meal,
But the food came cold and the drinks smelled old
And they both left hungry and hot.

- Brainstorm with learners how this new rhyme could be turned into a role play, news report, commercial, song, or any other idea. Have learners give suggestions. Act out or perform one or more of the suggestions with learners.
- Select a new nursery rhyme and go through the same steps of introducing, explaining and chorally repeating the rhyme with learners.
- Then put learners in pairs or small groups.
- Give each pair or small group a different category to focus on as they reimagine the nursery rhyme. Encourage learners to think of alternative ways to reimagine the rhymes, including as songs, chants, role plays, dialogues, commercials, news reports, or other.
- Circulate to give assistance and clarify directions.
- Give enough time for each pair or small group to have reimagined and practiced their new version of the nursery rhyme, then have them perform for the whole group without mentioning the category they were given.
- The whole group should guess what each pair's category was based on the performance.

Adaptations	<u>Make it easier</u> by modeling more rhymes and rhyme re-imagination with the whole group. Use categories that learners are familiar with and that you have discussed and done activities with in class. ptation<u>Make it harder</u> by doing less modeling and giving additional limitations on the re-imagination, such as needing to preserve the rhyme or giving categories that are more difficult to work with and more specific.
Remote Learning	This activity can easily be adapted to remote learning without any special modifications other than putting learners in rooms together. The choral repetition may be difficult on some platforms, but this can be mitigated by having learners repeat each one after the teacher. This helps to cement the intonation of the rhyme for the learners as they listen to it over and over again. You might also find online sites that contain the rhymes set to music or told by different characters.

5. Goose, Geese, Go!

Focus On	Reading, writing, with Listening and speaking for teams
Language Functions	Making statements, suggesting, asking questions
Grammar/ Vocabulary Practice	Irregular plural nouns or irregular verbs, or a mixture of both Vocabulary will depend on the content of squares on your grid.
LAF Aspects	<ul><li>Personal and meaningful: Learners are using their own knowledge and experience to create sentences.</li><li>Engaging: Learners are actively engaged as members of competitive teams.</li><li>Uses visuals: Pictures can be provided to go with the vocabulary; a grid is used as a graphic organizer.</li><li>Interactive: Learners interact with one another to complete the task.</li><li>Cooperative: Learners cooperate in teams by shouting out help.</li><li>Purposeful: There is a game to win.</li><li>Higher order thinking: Learners have to come up with sentences on their own.</li><li>Values diversity: Different experiences with the vocabulary in question will determine the sentences.</li></ul>
Primary HoM Practiced	Taking Responsible Risks, Communicating with Clarity and Precision, Striving for Accuracy, Finding Humor
Materials	The board or poster paper with a tic-tac-toe grid created on it where learners can write in each square.

This is a fun, action-packed, competitive team-based activity for classes that enjoy some physical movement and getting out of their seats as they practice language.

STEPS

- Create a large tic-tac-toe chart on the board with irregular verbs and/or irregular plural nouns, one in each square. See the example below.
- Split learners into two teams.
- Each team counts off separately so that each learner on each team has a number.
- The teacher calls out a number such as 3, and the 3's on each team rush to the board.
- They each write a full sentence in the square they choose using the noun in the plural form correctly. For example: The geese are in the lake, or I drank a whole bottle of water.
- The first learner who finishes with a correct sentence can add their X or O to their chosen square.
- The idea is to get three in a row, so the teams need to be strategic in what square they choose.
- The whole team can shout out help to the learner whose turn it is. To make it harder, require the sentences to be connected somehow to create a story, or have learners make increasingly longer sentences.
- A variation is to use irregular verbs instead of nouns in the square.
- Another, less hectic variation is to give each team a turn to come up.

Below is a sample grid to use:

Goose	Loaf	Man
Mouse	Child	Woman
Foot	Thief	Tooth

Adaptations	<u>Make it easier</u> by first going over the correct plural forms of the nouns or the correct forms of the irregular verbs in the past. Instead of competing in teams, have students work in pairs on a piece of paper with more time. <u>Make it harder</u> by not going over the correct plural forms of the nouns or the correct forms of the irregular verbs in the past. Have two or more tic-tac-toe grids going on the board with learners being able to choose any one they wish when their number is called. Impose a strict time limit.
Remote Learning	This activity can be adapted to remote learning by doing it in pairs with learners competing against one another, or small groups with two to a team. Another possibility is to use a website that allows learners to write on a board in real time such as ziteboard.com.

Chapter 9
LAF while Thinking about Thinking (Metacognition) & Communicating with Clarity and Precision

How often do we really think about our thinking? How often do we consider why we have certain ideas, opinions, or feelings? Metacognition is about allowing each of us to delve into our own ways of knowing and understanding the world and to realize where our thoughts and actions are coming from. Communicating with Clarity and Precision is the ability to impart those thoughts to others. Through thinking about our thinking, we gain awareness of ourselves within the context of the society and the culture we live in. By teaching our language learners to think about their own thinking, we are giving them the tools to further their understandings of themselves and their places in the world. By teaching them how to communicate their thoughts clearly, we are giving them the ability to present themselves to others in a way that is authentic. This is an especially important skill for language learners coming from diverse cultural and linguistic groups and from different ways of knowing and understanding the world around them. By practicing the HoM, Metacognition and Communicating with Clarity and Precision, we are empowering our learners to take learning into their own hands and giving them tools that will be valuable throughout their lives.

True Stories in TESOL

I spent a year teaching English in a language school in Fort Lauderdale, Florida, that offered language classes for part of the day, and leisure activities for the rest of the day. The learners were primarily young European adults, who were generally positive and happy people enjoying their time in Florida. However, they felt uncomfortable at the diner where they had lunch. The school was located on the second floor of a plaza and the diner was right underneath. In class they would often complain about the diner's wait staff, and it was becoming a problem because there was nowhere else they could eat and still keep the tight schedule they had at school.

I found my learners' complaints strange as I had been to the diner frequently for coffee before class, and had always found the wait staff to be quite friendly. One day I asked my learners for specific details about why they had trouble with the wait staff. At first my learners weren't sure how to explain the exact reasons they felt uncomfortable, so I asked them to spend a full minute thinking about it and imagining it in their heads. I wanted them to visualize the interactions they had at the diner in an attempt to identify the issue. After a minute, one of the learners hypothesized that it was the body language of the waitresses was the biggest problem. Others agreed and explained that the waitresses always looked annoyed with them and would sometimes roll their eyes. I asked my learners what provoked this behavior and they didn't know. They said they were ordering their meals, smiling and trying to be friendly but the waitresses still reacted this way.

I decided I would to a little investigation of my own and went down to the diner for coffee break that day while my learners were in another class. I struck up a conversation with one of the waitresses mentioning that I was a teacher at the language school. I had planned to casually ask her how she liked our learners, but I didn't have to. As soon as I told her I was a teacher, she said something along the lines of, "Ugh, I feel sorry for you." This surprised me very much and I asked her why. "Those guys are so rude," she said, "and they're here every day!" I told her that I found them very nice and asked her in what ways they were rude. She thought about it for a second and said that it was primarily two things. First, they ordered her around, and second they barely tipped.

I was not surprised at the fact they were barely tipping. Customary gratuity amounts vary across cultures, with some having no tipping at all. This was something I could plan a lesson on with my students, so they could better understand the local customs. I was surprised at the thought that the students were ordering the waitress around, so I asked her to be more specific about how this was happening. That is when the problem became clear. She said my students would order by saying, "Give me a coffee!" or "Give me a Coke!" as if she were a servant. The problem was revealed, and it was all about clarity in language! My learners were primarily German, and they were thinking in German. By beginning the sentence with "Give me...," they sounded demanding and rude, but my poor learners had no idea that this was the case. They were simply translating the way they would order in German.

Once I got back to classroom, I started a lesson on ordering in restaurants. It was all about using modals to be polite. Instead of, "Give me a coffee," we learned to say, "I'd like a coffee," or "Coffee, please." This slight change in language use completely changed the way the language was perceived. We also talked about tips and I found out they were tipping five to 10 percent. I explained that this was on the low side in the United States, and they were surprised. They had no idea. After that, there was no problem with the diner. In fact, the waitresses and the learners got along so well that they ended up becoming friends and socializing together on the weekends. Just a little bit of thinking and a little bit of clarifying precise language used worked wonders and added to my learners' opportunities to practice authentic language outside the classroom.

Techniques for the Classroom

If you went to nursery school or kindergarten in this country you may have had a teacher that asked you to "put your thinking cap on." I can clearly remember my teacher asking us to do that and all of us sitting in a circle and putting on an imaginary cap. It was a signal that it was time to think. I use a similar technique with my language learners. I don't literally ask them to put on a thinking cap, but I do ask them to do nothing but think at times. I give them time to thoroughly consider a problem or an idea before I ask them to answer a question or give a suggestion. I find that allowing students at all levels time to think, and do nothing else but think, produces more thoughtful responses from them once they are given a chance to talk or to write. It also encourages them to give others a chance to think before demanding a response to a request or a question. I believe this thinking time encourages more reflective students that work better both together and individually.

For language learners, thinking time can be an essential component of their progress in a second language. By thinking about their own thinking, learners become better acquainted with themselves while gaining the self-confidence and the cognitive flexibility to become great problem solvers in more than one language. In addition, extra time for thinking allows them to put their thoughts in order and thus formulate their communication so that it is more clear and precise.

1. Thinking Out Loud. One of the techniques that I like to employ on a regular basis with my learners is the technique of thinking out loud. When I am considering a problem that does not have an obvious or immediate answer and that is relevant to their lives, I allow them to hear what is going on in my head. I literally tell them what I am thinking by introducing my thinking process to them. I can start out by saying something like, "Let me think about this, let's see, so …the issue is… I am thinking that we might… or maybe we can…I think…" This technique of thinking out loud provides a model for them of how my thinking process is working and gives them the freedom to do the same thing with their thought process. It also provides for them a model of thinking in the language that I am helping them learn. They get to hear what thinking in that language sounds like, something they are not privy to in the real world, as we don't generally go around thinking out loud. On occasion, I ask my learners to share their thoughts just as I have shared mine. This helps them put into practice a thinking process in another language that they can eventually internalize to actually think in the second language rather than thinking in their L1 and translating in their heads before speaking.

2. Acknowledging Mistakes. One of the important things that I want my language learners to understand is that I make mistakes in my thinking just as they do. I often tell them of things that I used to think about language acquisition that were not necessarily correct. I talk to them about how I gained experience from failures or misunderstandings that helped me to change my thinking and to acquire more comprehensive or knowledge-based viewpoints. I also ask them to share mistakes that they made in their thinking in the past and talk about how their thinking has changed.

3. Free Writing. Sometimes it is easier to write about our thoughts than to say them out loud. However, writing for language learners can be a real challenge. I find that giving students five to 10 minutes to free write their thoughts at the beginning of a

day of lessons—with the caveat that I will not be reading what they write and they should not worry about grammar, vocabulary, or spelling—can help them to acknowledge their thinking and put it in to words. By further suggesting to language learners that they can write in both their native languages and in their target language, it gives the learners a chance to express themselves as developing bilinguals. We generally do not encourage language mixing and code switching in language classrooms, trying to focus as much as possible in the target language to develop that language. However, there is room for doing this some of the time and some value in opening the door for learners to use both of their languages to express themselves during activities such as free writing.

LAF in Class: Metacognition & Communicating with Clarity and Precision

1. Outside the Box

Language Skill Focus	Speaking, listening
Language Functions Practiced	Describing, explaining, hypothesizing, giving details
Grammar/Vocabulary Practiced	Declaratives, modals, adjectives, various tenses Vocabulary depends on the items chosen; household words such as spoon, plate, toilet paper, pen, towel, candle, soap, spatula, ironing board
Grouping Strategy	Individual, small group
LAF Aspects	• Personal and meaningful: Learners are giving their own ideas. • Engaging: Learners are actively engaged in the activity by guessing and surmising new roles for objects. • Uses visuals: Real objects are used throughout this activity. • Interactive: Learners interact with one another to complete the task. • Cooperative: Learners cooperate by building on one another's ideas. • Repetition: There is repetition and restating as they give their opinions and explanations. • Purposeful. The activity has a purpose outside of language use: coming up with a new use for an old item. • Higher order thinking: Learners have to come up with their own ideas for new and novel uses for known objects, inspiring creative thinking. • Values diversity: Different ways of thinking are valued and applauded during this activity.
Primary HoM Practiced	Metacognition, Thinking Flexibly, Creating, Imagining & Innovating, Communicating with Clarity & Precision

Materials Needed	For this activity you will use 'realia' also known as 'real stuff.' Get a box and fill it with different household items that are well known to learners, such as a spoon, a roll of toilet paper, a sock, a toothbrush, a hair tie, a straw, or any other collection of objects you can round up in your house and put in the box; you will also use paper and something to write with.

For this activity, language learners will be practicing thinking in new and different ways about items they are familiar with. This is a fun activity that engages the interest of learners and allows them to practice language in a low-risk environment where imagination is encouraged.

STEPS

- Explain to learners that you have a box full of items that they have all seen before.
- Ask them to guess what is in the box, explaining that you have things in the box that can be found in most homes. Depending on the language level of learners, you might want to create a word bank with the words they mention. If possible, create a semantic web so that the words they mention are in categories such as kitchen items, bathroom items, etc.
- As items are pulled out of the box, one by one, ask learner volunteers to first identify the item and then hypothesize about different purposes and uses for the item.
- If necessary, model this for your learners. For example, if a comb is pulled out of the box, identify it as an object used to comb hair. And then give a new purpose and use for a comb, such as using it as a back scratcher. Encourage learners to think of more ideas and uses for the comb.
- Proceed by pulling more items out of the box one by one and having learners either give their ideas individually or as a whole group, or work in pairs and then share with the whole group. Encourage as much imagination as possible.
- Ask learners to listen carefully to their classmates' ideas and build on those with new ideas, or use what a classmate said and extend that classmate's ideas.
- An extension of this activity can include having learners bring something from home that is specific to their culture to use in a follow up 'outside the box' game to be played with the class. Classmates need to guess the actual purpose of the object and then propose alternative purposes. This allows learners to share something about their home cultures or families with the entire class.
- A further extension could include writing up one of the items with a new purpose as if it were a new invention and creating a sales pitch for that item. This is best done in pairs and with learners who are at a high-intermediate to advanced level.

Adaptations	<u>Make it easier</u> by modeling more with more objects, giving students a word bank to use ahead of time that includes the vocabulary of the objects and descriptors, or giving them sentence starters for making their own sentences, such as, "This could be used as a…" or "This could be a…." <u>Make it harder</u> by asking learners to come up with more alternative uses or giving them limitations on those uses, such as requiring all uses to begin with the letter B or be something that can be done under water, etc.
Remote Learning	This activity can easily be adapted to remote learning by showing your learners the items in the box online, or using pictures of items that you find online.

2. Pro/Con

Language Skill Focus	Speaking, listening, variation with writing
Language Functions Practiced	Agreeing, disagreeing, giving opinions, contradicting, supporting
Grammar/Vocabulary Practiced	Declaratives, modals, past tense Vocabulary: Depending on the topics chosen, word banks can be provided for reference.
Grouping Strategy	Individual, whole group
LAF Aspects	• Personal and meaningful: Learners are giving their own opinions with their own words. • Engaging: Learners are actively engaged in the activity either as speakers or listeners. • Uses visuals: No visuals are used in this activity, but some could be added to give context with the categories. • Interactive: Learners interact with one another or the teacher in completing the task. • Cooperative: Learners cooperate by encouraging and shouting out hints to one another. • Repetition: There is repetition and restating as they give their opinions and explanations. • Higher order thinking: Learners have to think quickly and to take different opinions from their own while completing the activity. • Values diversity: Different ways of thinking are valued and applauded during this activity.
Primary HoM Practiced	Metacognition, Thinking Flexibly, Creating, Imagining & Innovating, Communicating with Clarity and Precision
Materials Needed	None required but it is a good idea to know ahead of time what topics you will want to review with your learner from your curriculum or any other topics that inspire different opinions. These could be traditionally controversial topics or any topic that you simply want them to think about and to recognize the multiple perspectives on that topic.

STEPS

- Start out by explaining to your learners that you will be playing a game called 'Pro/Con,' and ask them to hypothesize about what 'pro' means and what 'con' means.

- Explain that in this game 'pro' means to support something and 'con' means to not support something or to be against it, and that this is a fluency activity that will help them to practice using language quickly and continuously.

- Tell learners that you will be pulling a topic out of a hat (or anywhere else) and that they will have to say all of the ways they support that topic when you say 'pro' and then say everything they can think of against that topic when you say 'con.'

- Emphasize to learners that **whether or not they support the topic that is pulled is irrelevant**, they are practicing giving their opinions and support or non-support in two ways and **their true opinion should not be obvious** to anyone.

- Model this with an example topic, having a learner pull the topic and you as the teacher being in the 'hot seat.' When the learner says 'pro' you give all supportive comments, when the learner says 'con' you give all of your non-supportive comments. Make sure the learner switches between pro and con several times so that learners see how the game is played.

- Use plenty of fillers as you give your model such as, "Um, let me think … well, etc." Once you are finished with modeling, point these fillers out to learners and explain that native speakers often use fillers in their language when they are not sure what to say, and it is okay to use them. You may also ask them at this point about fillers in their own languages; these vary across cultures and languages. For example, in Spanish we do not say 'um' but we do say, 'e-e' and 'bueno.'

- The idea is to keep up a steady stream of talk using fillers as needed.

- It is a good idea to give the person in the hot seat about thirty seconds or so to think about the topic before starting with the pro/con sequence. I like to take turns with my learners so that they get to pro/con me as well on topics of their choice.

- A variation is to put learners in pairs to share being in hot seats. This takes pressure off of an individual learner but runs the danger of having one of the pair take over.

- Another variation is to do this as a writing activity with the whole class. Instead of having one at a time in the hot seat, all learners participate in writing their pros and cons as fast as they can as the teacher switches between the two. After that, pairs can exchange and compare papers or a whole class discussion can ensue.

The following is a partial transcription of a pro/con activity used with a small remote workshop for English language learners during the coronavirus pandemic. The topics chosen were from what was currently happening in the country (LAF: personal and meaningful) and included wearing masks, vaccines, opening businesses, going to parties, traveling, and going to school. You can create your own topics based on things you think your students will have opinions about or already have knowledge of and enjoy talking about.

T: The topic is WEARING A MASK. Pro!

LL: I think that it is a good idea to wear the mask. I think everyone should wear mask because of the corona, it is a virus dangerous. We need to wear a mask to be the protect of the others. We do not want to…I don't know….I think we wear mask to protect of all the peoples….it…

T: Con!

LL: I do not want to wear a mask! Why I should wear a mask when the other people don't wear no mask! A mask is not protect me at all. It is not nice to wear a mask. To wear a mask is ….it is not good….because, em. I am thinking it…because, em…it is not a nice to do? I think…

T: Pro!

LL: Wear a mask! Why you don't want to wear a mask you people? You are make the virus spreading and more danger for every person. I always wear a mask. I have a mask that I make with my sock. It is easy to make and everybody can do it…I can show you how to do it. It is a good thing because the mask is protect you and also it is protect me….um…we need to love the other person …

T: Con!

LL: Don't tell me what to do government! I am a free person and I don't like to stop my breath with the mask. It feels bad on my face. The mask look ugly. It is too hot for a mask, I can't almost breathe with the mask….the mask is stupid…

This is a partial section of the transcript of this learner who is at an intermediate level of English. This activity caused plenty of laughing in addition to language practice as learners had to go back and forth and support an opinion that they did not actually hold. It also led to honest and enthusiastic discussion about current events and engaged the learners in using language to express their feelings. Pro/Con provides an interesting way to clarify thinking on a variety of topics and get a good handle on any misunderstanding of content or lack of knowledge that is being studied, because it allows us to actually hear the thought process.

Adaptations	<u>Make it easier</u> by modeling more and switching to pro or con when you see a learner is having trouble thinking of more things to say. You can also provide a word bank with fillers and vocabulary integral to your topics or sentence starters. <u>Make it harder</u> by switching between pro and con rapidly and not switching when you see that a learner is running out of things to say, forcing them to come up with more things. You can also make it harder by choosing topics that there is little doubt about whether or not to support so that con becomes very difficult or vice versa.
Remote Learning	This activity can easily be adapted to remote learning without any special modifications.

3. Back to Back Drawing Challenge

Language Skill Focus	Listening, speaking
Language Functions Practiced	Explaining, describing, giving directions, asking and answering questions
Grammar/Vocabulary Practiced	Commands, simple present, comparatives, prepositional phrases Vocabulary will depend on challenge prompts, but will include direction words, shapes, sizes, and prepositions such as over, under, next to, in, on, etc.
Grouping Strategy	Pairs
LAF Aspects	<ul><li>Personal and meaningful: Learners get to describe their own creations.</li><li>Engaging: Learners generally enjoy this activity because it is hands on.</li><li>Interactive: There is no way to do this without interacting.</li><li>Cooperative: They must cooperate to complete the activity.</li><li>Purposeful: Learners must complete a design.</li><li>Repetition: There is natural repetition during this activity.</li><li>Higher order thinking: Learners must think outside the box to describe objects.</li></ul>
Primary HoM Practiced	Communicating with Clarity & Precision, Striving for Accuracy, Questioning and Problem Posing
Materials Needed	Paper, pencils, folders

STEPS

- Have learners sit back to back if you have an even number, or take turns working with one of them if you have an odd number. The drawings used should be relatively simple line drawings. An example is included on the following page.
- One member of each pair gets a closed folder with a drawing inside. The other member of the pair gets a piece of paper and a writing instrument.
- The person with the drawing needs to describe it in as much detail as possible (using the HoMs Communicating with Clarity and Precision and Striving for Accuracy) so that his or her partner can replicate the drawing on their piece of paper.
- You may wish to model the activity first with the whole group by describing a drawing only you can see and having the whole class try to replicate it, encouraging learners to ask you questions and being as detailed as possible.
- In the back-to-back pairs, the listener has a blank sheet of paper and needs to listen carefully to his or her partner to know exactly what to draw on that paper. The idea is for the drawings to be as similar as possible.
- For this to increase in benefit as a language learning activity, the listener should be encouraged to ask questions for clarity and ask for as much clarification and repetition as needed.
- The only rule is for each member of the pair to refrain from looking at the other's paper.
- A variation is to have a structure that one builds with Cuisinaire rods or Legos and the partner has to build an exact replica with the same materials simply through listening to the description of what has been built.
- This activity can easily be adapted for different ages and levels of learners, but you may have to add a blindfold for the listener if the learners are very young as the temptation to look at what the partner has on paper is great.

Adaptations	Make it easier by sticking to very simple drawings and giving learners a bank of vocabulary that is useful, such as straight, longer, shorter, middle, curve, corner, etc. Make it harder by having learners draw more detailed drawings or providing them yourself. Do not give a word bank, and/or set a time limit for rapid completion.
Remote Learning	This activity is easily adapted for remote learning. Just make sure that only one learner can see the visual you provide and the other must listen to recreate it.

4. Thinking Bubbles

Language Skill Focus	Reading, writing, speaking, listening
Language Functions Practiced	Functions will vary according to the images chosen but could include the following: asking and answering questions, describing, giving commands, complaining, and persuading.
Grammar/Vocabulary Practiced	Interrogatives, simple present, adjectives, exclamations Vocabulary depends on the images chosen; a brainstorm for needed vocabulary can precede the activity.
Grouping Strategy	Individual, small group
LAF Aspects	• Personal and meaningful: Learners are working with their own images. • Engaging: Learners are actively engaged in the activity by creating the thinking bubbles. • Uses visuals: Pictures are provided by teachers and learners. • Interactive: Learners interact with one another to complete the task. • Cooperative: Learners cooperate in small groups or pairs to complete the activity. • Repetition: There is repetition and restating as they give their opinions and explanations. • Higher order thinking: Learners have to come up with a their own ideas for the thinking bubbles. • Values diversity: Different ways of seeing the world are inherent in the activity, and learners can provide their own family photographs.
Primary HoM Practiced	Metacognition, Thinking Flexibly, Finding Humor, Communicating with Clarity & Precision
Materials Needed	Personal photographs provided by teacher and students, or cut out pictures from magazines, book illustrations, online art or other sources that tell a story. Large pieces of poster paper or newsprint, markers, crayons and/or paint.

For this activity, learners first look at different pictures or illustrations of people in various situations and imagine what they might be thinking at the moment that has been captured by the photographer or artist. It can provide a way to review anything you have been talking about with learners and allow them to share their family stories with the class.

STEPS

- Bring in personal photographs and/or ask learners to bring in photos and images that are important to them and that feature people.
- Ideally, photos should have only one to three people in them and faces should be easily seen. This is not essential but it usually makes the activity easier.
- Explain to learners that you will be putting thought bubbles on the people in the pictures, imagining what those people are thinking. Model by using a picture of your own and the thought bubbles that you have imagined.
- Have learners complete this activity working in pairs to help one another out with their photographs.
- Split the class in two, making sure you keep pairs who worked together on the same side.
- Collect the photographs and the thinking bubbles from half the class without keeping the thinking bubbles and photographs together. Give these items in two separate containers to the other half of the class.
- Do this with both halves of the class, so each ends up with the pictures and thought bubbles that were created by learners in the other half.
- Have learners try to match the pictures with the thought bubbles. Encourage plenty of interaction and explanation among learners to find the right fit.
- If the class is very large, it is better to do this in small groups rather than halves, with ideally no more than six learners in each group.
- Have learners share their ideas about which thoughts go with which images with the whole class and see if they were right or wrong.

Adaptations	Make it easier by modeling more with your own pictures or pictures in magazines. Have learners practice in pairs with several given pictures before using their own pictures; provide a word bank that will help them with short expressions, phrases and sentence starters.
	Make it harder by providing learners with more complicated images that are related to one another, such as images in magazines all featuring a certain event, and asking them to put the images in an order with thought bubbles in each that relate to one another.

Remote Learning	This activity can easily be adapted to remote learning by showing your learners the examples you have developed remotely and giving them time to gather a picture or two in their houses, then proceeding with the activity. You can also provide pictures for them to work with by displaying these and doing this activity as a whole group. You would continue the activity by having each learner send you their picture with thought bubbles and you would redistribute these, unattached, to other learners by dividing your online class in halves or small groups and providing pictures and thought bubbles to each group. Make sure that students do not end up in a group that includes their own pictures or thought bubbles.

5. Dictation Situation

Language Skill Focus	Listening, writing, reading and speaking extensions
Language Functions Practiced	Restating, describing, hypothesizing, guessing
Grammar/Vocabulary Practiced	This is dependent on the grammar in the dictation stories chosen. Vocabulary depends on stories chosen.
Grouping Strategy	Individual, small group, whole group
LAF Aspects	<ul><li>Personal and meaningful: This is possible if dictations that students can connect to are chosen.</li><li>Engaging: Learners are actively engaged in the activity by listening and then problem solving.</li><li>Interactive: Learners interact with one another while problem solving.</li><li>Cooperative: Learners cooperate in small groups or pairs to complete the activity.</li><li>Repetition: There is repetition and restating as learners give their opinions and explanations.</li><li>Higher order thinking: Learners have to solve a problem.</li><li>Values diversity: Different perspectives and methods of problem solving are present.</li></ul>
Primary HoM Practiced	Communicating with Clarity & Precision, Striving for Accuracy, Metacognition, Thinking Flexibly
Materials Needed	Paragraph-long riddles, short mysteries or other short paragraphs that have a hidden problem or challenge. Several examples are given below. One website to find mystery riddles: https://www.riddlesandanswers.com/tag/mystery-riddles/#ixzz6bRvUojYt

STEPS

- Choose one learner to dictate a short paragraph with a story or riddle that contains a problem that needs to be solved. Another option is to dictate the paragraph yourself first.

- All other learners take dictation.

- Next, have a second learner dictate the paragraph so that the other learners can check their work and the original reader can take dictation.

- Finally, have a third learner dictate the paragraph for a third and final check.

- Pair up learners, or put them in small cooperative groups.

- Learner pairs or small groups should check their dictated paragraphs to see if they all look the same, and make any revisions necessary.

- Have learners work together to resolve the problem or the riddle contained in the paragraph.

- Circulate among learners to check progress and check for correct answers.

- The first group or pair to finish with the correct answer is the winner.

Below are examples of paragraphs that can be used for this activity. For more see the website above, or create your own.

Example 1:

This is an unusual paragraph. I'm curious as to just how quickly you can find out what is so unusual about it. It looks so ordinary and plain that you would think nothing was wrong with it. In fact, nothing is wrong with it! It is highly unusual though. Study it and think about it, but you still may not find anything odd. But if you work at it a bit, you might find out.

Answer: There are no 'E's in the paragraph even though E is the most commonly used letter in the English language.

Example 2:

A man leaves a $100,000 dollar bill on his desk and leaves for work. When he returns, the money has disappeared. He has three suspects: the cook, the cleaner, and the delivery man. The cook says she put the money under a book on his desk to keep it safe. They check and it is no longer there. The cleaner says she moved it to the inside of the book between page one and two while she was cleaning. They open the book and look between page one and two and it isn't there. The delivery man says he saw the money sticking out of the book and to keep it safe he moved it to between pages two and three. Once they are done the culprit is promptly arrested. Who did it and how did they know?

Answer: If they look between pages one and two and the money isn't there, it means that page three has page two on the other side of it, so there is no way to put money in between pages two and three and the delivery man must be lying.

Adaptations	<u>Make it easier</u> by reading the story to your students three times, then ask learners to read it to one another in pairs. <u>Make it harder</u> by having learners only do the dictation. Include longer dictations with more complex vocabulary and grammar for a bigger challenge.
Remote Learning	This activity can easily be adapted to remote learning with no significant modifications other than putting learners in small groups or pairs in separate virtual rooms to complete the activity.

Chapter 10
LAF while Questioning and Problem Posing/ Striving for Accuracy

One of the signs of being a good thinker and scholar is the ability to ask interesting and relevant questions. Most language teachers strive to create an environment where questions are welcome as part of the learning process and where they have as much validity, or even more validity in many cases, than do answers. A great question will always lead to more questions and thus to more possibilities for critical and creative thinking with language interaction.

In order to create this kind of climate of questioning, it is important that we resist the temptation to answer all of our learners' questions – even when we know the answers. Rather than giving our learners the answers to all of the questions they ask us, we can enhance the learning experience by giving them a chance to answer one another's questions, and teaching them questioning and problem posing skills. Guiding our learners in how to ask good questions will help to prepare them for extended interactions with native speakers and others in the target language.

True Stories of TESOL

When I was teaching a group of language learners in a Florida language school, I had an experience that reminded me to give my students and myself time to think and formulate questions. One day, one of my Italian students asked me to tell them the most important thing they should know about English language pronunciation so that they could sound like native speakers. I was not sure how to answer this question. I did not want my learners to focus too much on their pronunciation or worry about it because I found that when they did, they were less likely to interact. However, I did want to give them useful information and answer their questions.

"Let me think about that a bit," I said, "we can get back to it at the end of the class." That answer seemed to satisfy my student, and we went on with the class. I was hoping he would forget about his question at the end of class, but he did not, repeating his question and putting me on the spot. I began by emphasizing to him and the whole class that they should not focus too much on whether or not they sounded like native speakers, but rather on whether they were understandable and able to communicate competently.

My student answered me in the following way, "But teacher, would you rather sound like a native speaker or be understandable?" I admitted that I would rather sound like a native speaker and countered with, "Would you rather worry about how you sound or learn more ways to communicate effectively?" He admitted that he would rather learn more. We went back and forth like this for a while inspiring a "Would you rather...?" activity that we spontaneously created as a class and that I will include in the activities in this chapter. This also reminded me of Jazz Chants (Graham, 2000) that can be used to practice pronunciation and are fun and engaging. We incorporated those chants very successfully into our classes. At the end of the day this student helped me to create a new activity and remember an old one to the benefit of the whole class. This occurred because I did not answer his question right away, allowing learners to come up with more questions, and giving the whole class practice in interacting and forming interesting questions.

Techniques for the Classroom

1. <u>What to Why?</u> We often use the question 'what' in our teaching and learning activities. What did the character say? What happened next? What is the name of the state capitol? These and many more 'what' questions tend to dominate teaching activities and keep the level of thinking at the lower levels of Bloom's taxonomy (for information on Bloom's taxonomy see Anderson, et. al 2001). I suggest that we put more of a focus on 'why.' When we let 'why' drive our questioning strategies, we encourage critical thinking and extended language use. This technique allows learners to find the 'what' along the way as they are exploring the 'why.' For example, "Why did the character make the statement?" By asking this question, a learner will be more analytical and critical and also need to know what the character said in order to answer why he or she said it. At the same time, more language is used to answer the question.

2. <u>Asking Big Questions:</u> In addition to encouraging learners to ask interesting questions and asking interesting questions ourselves, we also need to ask big, broad and more-than-one-right-answer questions. Big questions invite inquiry and exploration while inspiring curiosity and creativity. According to Johnston (2012), uncertainty encourages dialogue, whereas certainty limits learning. Therefore, big questions provide prolonged interactive language practice opportunities.

3. <u>Validating multiple perspectives</u>: When learners are in classroom environments that encourage more-than-one-right-answer questions and different ways of thinking about an issue, they are more likely to keep an open mind and value cultural experiences and perspectives that differ from their own. They realize that each of us sees the world in our own unique way, and that each of these ways is valid. In order to value multiple perspectives we have to give our language learners a chance to encounter questions that are difficult to answer linguistically, and that include dilemmas, predicaments and conundrums. This, in turn, gives them the enhanced ability to work collaboratively with others, negotiate meaning through discourse and gaining further interactive opportunities.

LAF in Class Activities:
Questioning and Problem Posing & Striving for Accuracy

1. The Catch-All Bag

Language Skill Focus	Speaking, listening
Language Functions Practiced	Asking questions, making predictions, guessing
Grammar/Vocabulary Practiced	Interrogatives, adjectives Vocabulary depends on the pictures of the items in the bag; teacher can provide a word bank and question starters to help students formulate questions.
Grouping Strategy	Individual, whole group
LAF Aspects	<ul><li>Personal and meaningful: Learners are asking their own questions.</li><li>Engaging: Learners are actively engaged in the activity by guessing what is in the bag.</li><li>Uses visuals: Pictures are used throughout this activity.</li><li>Interactive: Learners interact with one another to complete the task by listening and not repeating one another's questions.</li><li>Cooperative: Learners cooperate by building on one another's information and learning from one another.</li><li>Purposeful: Learners need to find out what is in the bag, something they don't already know.</li><li>Repetition: There is repetition as they continuously use question words.</li><li>Higher order thinking: Learners have to come up with their own ideas for what is hidden based on the information they are hearing.</li><li>Values diversity: Different ways of questioning are valued and can stem from learner's background experiences and knowledge.</li></ul>
Primary HoM Practiced	Questioning and Problem Posing, Striving for Accuracy, Metacognition, Thinking Flexibly, Communicating with Clarity and Precision

Materials Needed	For this activity you will use photographs of well-known people, places or things. These can be familiar to students from their study or actual experience. Using political figures and celebrities mixed with places and things helps to keep the activity fun and engaging. You will also need paper lunch bags for hiding the pictures.

STEPS

- For this activity, learners need to ask a series of questions to determine what is hidden inside of a bag.
- Gather paper lunch bags or envelopes that allow you to hide pictures inside. You may use pictures of people, places, or things that you want your learners to ask questions about in order to guess what or who is in the bag. These pictures can be from something that they have studied or are currently studying, including readings or cultural information. Using pictures of celebrities and locations is also a good idea.
- Tell learners that you have something or someone in the bag, but you can't tell them what or who it is. They have to ask a series of questions to figure out what is in the bag.
- Set some ground rules, such as that they can't ask directly what it is and that they have to ask at least five to 10 questions before guessing. This is an important rule, as many learners will jump straight to guessing rather than asking questions to narrow down what could be in the bag.
- Let learners know that the thing in the bag is a picture of something so they shouldn't necessarily go by the size or shape of the bag in composing their questions.
- Start off by modeling the activity first with a picture of a common item such as a spoon or a fork so they get the hang of it. In my experience learners enjoy this activity very much and want to do it often.
- Each learner gets to ask one question at a time giving each learner a chance to ask a question until someone wants to make a guess. No guessing until at least five questions have been asked.
- If a learner guesses and is wrong, the learner may be 'out' or you can keep them in the activity.
- You might want to use a questioning strategy so that you learn more by the answers to the questions. For example, you can ask questions about categories such as: Is it living? Is it male or female? Is it an animal? A food?

Adaptations	Make it easier by going over many examples with them and using easily guessed items. Provide hints and scaffolding as needed. Make it harder by using very specific pictures of items that are not commonly guessed, such as a two-toed sloth or a location that is remote. Add to the stakes by giving a time limit.
Remote Learning	This activity can easily be adapted to remote learning without any special modifications.

2. Intriguing Interviews

Language Skill Focus	Speaking and listening with possible writing extension
Language Functions Practiced	Asking questions, making predictions, guessing, denying, asserting, emphasizing
Grammar/Vocabulary Practiced	Interrogatives, adjectives, conditionals, modals Vocabulary depends on the interview subjects and topics. A word and phrase bank can be provided to help learners.
Grouping Strategy	Pairs, whole group
LAF Aspects	<ul><li>Personal and meaningful: Learners are asking their own questions.</li><li>Engaging: Learners are actively engaged in interviews as the interviewer or interviewee.</li><li>Uses visuals: Videos and body language serve as the visuals.</li><li>Interactive: Learners interact with one another to complete the task by participating in interviews.</li><li>Cooperative: Learners cooperate by interviewing one another in pairs.</li><li>Purposeful: Learners conduct an interview and find out things they did not already know.</li><li>Repetition: There is repetition as they ask questions and follow ups.</li><li>Higher order thinking: Learners have to come up with their own questions and answers.</li><li>Values diversity: Different ways of questioning are valued and can stem from a learner's background experiences and knowledge.</li></ul>
Primary HoM Practiced	Questioning and Problem Posing, Striving for Accuracy, Metacognition, Thinking Flexibly, Communicating with Clarity and Precision
Materials Needed	Pictures of famous people or famous characters from literature or history that students are familiar with. Short videos on YouTube that show a famous person being interviewed.

STEPS

- Begin by watching an interesting and short video clip of a famous person being interviewed. There are many such interviews on YouTube. Find one that you know will be intriguing to your specific learners. Make sure that it is short, or use only a few minutes of a longer interview.
- After watching the video, ask learners to try to remember the questions that the interviewer asked and list those on a board or a piece of paper.
- Brainstorm ways to make those questions more interesting.
- Model this with your learners by showing them how to improve on a question or on a follow up question. For example, take the question, "What was it like to star in this movie?" and change it to, "Describe the most challenging moment for you while you were making the movie. How did you feel and how did you get through it?"
- Ask learners why the second question is more interesting. Help them to notice that it asks for more detail and that it helps the interviewee focus on an answer.
- Next, select a famous person or a character from literature or history. For younger learners, it may be a good idea to choose superheroes or princesses.
- Next, have learners exchange characters or people, so that they can interview one another.
- Each learner has the job of interviewing the person or character that was chosen by asking at least five or more interesting questions.
- Encourage learners to ask follow up questions after hearing their partners' responses.
- Perform interviews for the whole class.
- A variation is to allow class members to ask follow up questions or alternative questions to the interviewee, or to pass written questions to the interviewer to ask.

Adaptations	Make it easier by modeling interviews with volunteer students and starting with easy questions.
	Make it harder by giving interviewers directions with information they need to obtain that is difficult to get, and tell interviewees which information they should not reveal or that they want to reveal and to be questioned about. These two sets of directions should oppose one another to make the interview more challenging.
Remote Learning	This activity can easily be adapted to remote learning without any special modifications. Students can be separated into pairs in remote rooms to practice their interviews, then return to the class to perform.

3. Real Life Mysteries

Language Skill Focus	Reading, speaking and listening
Language Functions Practiced	Asking questions, making predictions, guessing
Grammar/Vocabulary Practiced	Interrogatives, adjectives Vocabulary depends on the mysteries you choose, but could include words that are pertinent to many mysteries, such as suspicious, unknown, witness, alibi, etc.
Grouping Strategy	Pairs, whole group
LAF Aspects	• Personal and meaningful: Learners are asking their own questions. • Engaging: Learners are actively engaged in interviews as interviewer or interviewee. • Uses visuals: Videos and body language serve as the visuals. • Interactive: Learners interact with one another to complete the task by participating in interviews. • Cooperative: Learners cooperate by interviewing one another in pairs. • Purposeful: Learners have a mystery to solve. • Repetition: There is repetition as they ask questions and follow ups. • Higher order thinking: Learners have to come up with their own questions and answers. • Values diversity: Different ways of questioning are valued and can stem from a learner's background experiences and knowledge.
Primary HoM Practiced	Questioning and Problem Posing, Striving for Accuracy, Metacognition, Thinking Flexibly, Communicating with Clarity & Precision
Materials Needed	A mystery box with newspaper clippings or partially printed websites featuring real-life unsolved mysteries, small 'evidence' journals and something to write with.

STEPS

- During this activity, students put on their detective hats and try to solve real-life mysteries. There are many online resources that can be used to find mysteries; select a few to print out and put in the mystery box.
- It is best if each mystery comes with accompanying pictures and/or some kind of evidence, and each is in a labeled envelope in your mystery box (any shoebox or other box will do).
- Have a student randomly choose one envelope without looking inside the box.
- Have the student read the mystery to the whole class, and share any accompanying visuals or evidence.
- Encourage students to write the key ideas down on their papers or have the student who chose the mystery write the key facts on the board.
- Put students in small groups to hypothesize about what might have happened and to create a list of questions that you would ask if you were to investigate this mystery.
- Finally, have students conduct mock investigations with 'witnesses' or 'experts' that could help them solve the mystery. This part will take some imagination on the part of the witnesses.
- In groups of four to six, one learner may play the part of the detective, another student or two can be witnesses, another an expert, and so on.
- As a closing activity learners must come up with their supported solution to the mystery based on their questions and understanding of the event.
- An extension can include time for the students to look online for what other people think happened and compare it with their own solutions.

One mystery I have used with learners is that of DB Cooper the hijacker. The description and directions are below.

In 1971 an unidentified man – referred to as DB Cooper in the media, based on the alias he used – hijacked a plane on a flight from Portland to Seattle. He demanded $200,000 in ransom, a fuel truck standing by in Seattle to refuel the plane upon landing, and four parachutes. If he didn't get what he asked for, he said he would blow up the plane with a bomb he claimed to have in his luggage. He got everything he asked for. The plane he was travelling on was emptied of passengers, and only the hijacker and crew remained. At some point in the flight, the man clutched his case full of money and jumped off the plane. Although the FBI tried for years to track him down, no trace of this man was ever found, nor was his real name ever discovered. Nobody knows why he hijacked the plane or where he ended up. No body was ever recovered.

1. Read the unsolved mystery and brainstorm on what might have happened.
2. Come up with five to 10 questions that you could ask to try to find the solution to this mystery. Think about individuals you would choose to interview and how you would ask the questions.
3. What other questions might you ask to help you find a solution? Think of questions you could research and imagine what information you might obtain.
4. Ask questions of your 'witness' or 'expert' and record their responses in your journal.
5. Come up with your solution to the mystery and write it down or act it out with your partners.

Adaptations	Make it easier by providing short and easy-to-solve mysteries with plenty of modeling, known vocabulary and familiar grammar. You may also give each cooperative group a copy of the directions and the mystery written out. Make it harder: by providing longer and more complex mysteries. A time limit can also pose a greater challenge.
Remote Learning	This activity can easily be adapted to remote learning without any special modifications. Students can be separated into small groups in remote rooms to conduct their investigations, then return to the class to share their conclusions. In the case of remote learning, real mysteries with online solutions should not be used as students will tend to Google the solutions.

4. Would you rather...?

Focus On	Speaking, listening, reading and writing
Language Functions	Rationalizing, explaining, considering, predicting, describing
Grammar/Vocabulary Practice	Conditionals, modals, comparatives Vocabulary depends on the topics chosen. Give vocabulary word banks and sentence starters to lower level learners.
Grouping Strategy	Pairs
LAF Aspects	• Personal and meaningful: Learners are asking their own questions. • Engaging: Learners are actively engaged in interviews as interviewer or interviewee. • Uses visuals: Videos and body language serve as the visuals. • Interactive: Learners interact with one another to complete the task by participating in interviews. • Cooperative: Learners cooperate by interviewing one another in pairs. • Purposeful: Learners teach about themselves and learn about others in the class. • Repetition: There is repetition as they ask questions and follow ups. • Higher order thinking: Learners have to come up with their own questions and answers. • Values diversity: Different ways of questioning are valued and can stem from a learner's background experiences and knowledge.
Materials Needed	Index cards with moral/ethical questions on them that can come from your curriculum, current events or any other source. Pen, paper and optional response forms that give learners a guide for how to structure their answers and what is expected of them. A model for this type of form is provided, as well as sample questions to put on the index cards. There are online websites that provide ethical questions.

STEPS

- Create cards beforehand that feature "Would you rather...?" questions that are thought provoking and that demand critical and creative thinking skills. The cards should also keep in mind the age, interests and language level of the students.
- Break up learners into pairs or small groups.
- The activity proceeds with one learner choosing a card from the pile and reading it out loud. Everyone else has a chance to hear the question and think about his or her own response to the question.
- Try to implement a one-minute thinking time limit before writing can begin.
- Next, each language learner and teacher writes his or her response to the question along with a short explanation of why he or she thinks that way. In addition, each person writes **what they believe their partners will say**.
- Model this for your learners by going first. A limited amount of time should be given for writing the responses that guarantees enough time to write a thoughtful response but doesn't give an excessive amount of time.
- Next, each person reads what he or she thinks one of the others has said in their response.
- One person is focused on at a time. That person will then read his or her response. A conversation may follow about how close or far from each person's response the others were and how each person's thinking process can be different and yet they may arrive at the same conclusions. Responses vary widely, and the thinking behind those responses can be examined and analyzed.
- Continue with each person choosing one question from the pile and proceeding with the thinking, writing, and guessing of responses. The harder the questions are, the more time and thought the activity should take.
- I like to throw in at least one silly question for every two or three very serious questions to lighten the mood and see how we each find humor in different situations. If you are teaching a group of five or more learners, I suggest you limit the questions to two or three for each time you do the activity. Writing out the responses and discussing responses for so many people takes up quite a bit of time if it is done thoughtfully.

Response Form

Questions	What I would rather and why….	What I think you would rather and why…
1.		
2.		
3.		
4.		
5.		
6.		
7.		
8.		
9.		
10.		
11.		
12.		

Sample Question Cards:

Would you rather follow laws you think are stupid or break them if you don't think you'd get caught?	Would you rather lie or tell the truth when the truth would hurt someone's feelings?	Would you rather marry someone who loves you more than you love them or marry someone you love more than they love you?
Would you rather be a dog or a cat?	Would you rather have one good friend for life or many friends that come and go?	Would you rather only eat at restaurants the rest of your life or at home if you had to choose one?
Would you rather be a child or an adult?	Would you rather change your personality or your appearance?	Would you rather be living now or a hundred years from now?

Adaptations	<u>Make it easier</u> by modeling several questions for your learners and by giving them sentence starters for response such as: I would…I think he would…because… <u>Make it harder</u> by giving less time for thinking before responding, include questions that demand more complex language and provide less modeling.
Remote Learning	This activity can easily be adapted to remote learning without any special modifications. Students can be separated into pairs by using waiting rooms in online meeting spaces.

5. Liar, Liar, Pants on Fire!

Focus On	Speaking, listening and reading
Language Functions	Rationalizing, explaining, considering, predicting, describing
Grammar/Vocabulary Practice	Conditionals, modals, comparatives Vocabulary depends on the topics chosen. Give vocabulary word banks and sentence starters to lower level learners.
Grouping Strategy	Pair, whole group
LAF Aspects	<ul><li>Personal and meaningful: Learners are creating their own narratives and explanations.</li><li>Engaging: Learners are actively engaged in trying to defend or reveal a lie or a truth.</li><li>Uses visuals: Body language and images can serve as the visuals.</li><li>Interactive: Learners interact with one another to complete the task by participating in interviews.</li><li>Cooperative: Learners cooperate by working together to reveal a lie or defend a truth.</li><li>Purposeful: Learners accumulate fun facts.</li><li>Repetition: There is repetition as classmates ask questions and follow ups.</li><li>Higher order thinking: Learners have to come up with their own reasons for why something is true.</li><li>Values diversity: Different ways of questioning are valued and can stem from a learner's background experiences and knowledge.</li></ul>
Materials Needed	A collection of odd facts and myths; some will be true and some will be false. Samples are provided below.

STEPS

- Pair up learners and explain that they will be doing an activity where they have to guess whether the facts are truths or lies.
- Distribute either a TRUTH or a LIE to each pair of learners.
- Each pair discusses their fact and comes up with at least three supporting reasons that 'prove' their fact is true, whether or not it is true. Half of the pairs will have a lie, but they need to pretend that it is true and convince the whole class.
- Pairs present their fact to the class and explain why it is true. Allow classmates to ask questions. Learners either have to make up facts to answer the questions, or use facts that they already know to convince the rest of the class that they are telling the truth.
- Class members discuss and come to an agreement, if possible, about whether they have heard a truth or a lie. If they think the pair is telling a lie, the class shouts out, "Liar, liar pants on fire!" If the class agrees that the pair is telling the truth, they shout out, "We believe you!"
- If the class is correct and the pair of students have told a lie then the class wins. If the pair was telling the truth then the pair wins that round.

TRUTHS

- A crocodile cannot stick its tongue out.
- A shrimp's heart is in its head.
- It is physically impossible for pigs to look up into the sky.
- Wearing headphones for just an hour could increase the bacteria in your ear by 700 times.
- Everyone's tongue print is different.
- A shark is the only known fish that can blink with both eyes.
- "Dreamt" is the only English word that ends in the letters "mt."
- Kangaroos cannot walk backwards.
- Snails can nap for up to three years.
- Some perfumes contain whale poop.

LIES

- In an average lifetime, you might eat around 25 assorted insects while you are alseep. (This number is actually 70.)
- Some lipsticks contain octopus blood.
- Cat urine is good for fighting the common cold.
- The average human dream lasts only two to three seconds.
- There are 100 ways to make change for a dollar. (That numbers is actually 293.)
- Almonds are part of the tomato family. (They are actually members of the peach family)
- There are only three words in the English language that end in "dous": tremendous, horrendous, stupendous. (There are actually 4: hazardous.)
- A cow has 32 muscles in each ear. (Actually a cat does.)
- Hippopotamus milk is purple. (It is actually pink.)
- Nails grow faster in the heat. (They actually grow faster in the cold.)

Adaptations	Make it easier by modeling several truth and lie facts for your learners, and making sure that they understand all of the vocabulary in the truths and lies.

Make it harder by giving less time and turning it from a pair activity to an individual activity; give more obscure truths and lies or have learners come up with their own. |
| **Remote Learning** | This activity can easily be adapted to remote learning without any special modifications. Learners can be separated in to pairs by using waiting rooms in online meeting spaces. |

Chapter 11
LAF with Creating, Imagining & Innovating/ Responding with Wonderment and Awe

Creativity is the highest level of thinking, according to the revised version of Bloom's Taxonomy. We know that in the rapidly changing world we live in, with constant new technologies available, people who can think creatively have a distinct advantage. While we are focused on helping our language learners improve their skills in language, we must also be focused on helping them do so in a manner that allows for creativity. If we ensure that our learners are given activities and environments that inspire creativity, we can also be assured that they will acquire more complex and multilayered language that will engage them and keep them motivated to learn.

In addition to encouraging creativity, innovation and imagination, we can also encourage our learners to respond with wonderment and awe. This is a skill that we do not need to worry about with small children. The whole world presents opportunities for them to experience wonderment and awe. They are in a constant state of being amazed and thrilled by things that we older learners consider normal or passé. Yet, when we do experience the sense of wonder, it is something that sticks with us. By creating and utilizing activities that inspire a sense of wonderment and awe, we are giving language learners experiences in the target language that are memorable and meaningful. Research indicates that these types of experiences, especially those that trigger emotional responses, are more likely to be retained (Swain, 2013). We can surmise that the language that surrounds these experiences is more likely to be remembered.

In creative and flexible language learning environments, learners are encouraged to 'play' with language. They are free to discover and enjoy the process of language acquisition much in the spirit of first language acquirers. In the classroom, this playing can take the form of games, role-playing activities, simulations, and engaging task-based experiences such as scavenger hunts and mysteries. Other learners and the teacher become collaborators and sometimes competitors. As language teachers, we are preparing our learners to be able to face any challenge in the target language, including being able to live, work, and socialize in that language. By including creativity, innovation, imagination and wonderment in activities we use in the classroom, we are not only making our classrooms more interesting, we are also supplying our students with the skills they need to encounter any difficulties they face outside of the classroom.

When I think back to my own experiences as a language learner, there is no doubt that creativity and wonderment had a lot to do with how much and how fast I learned. When I first came from Argentina to the U.S. at the age of four, my mother was completing her medical residency. Because of this she had very little time to care for me, and for several months I spent many hours a day with a wonderful young French woman who was my babysitter. Mireille spoke neither Spanish nor English. Therefore, I presume she spoke to me in French. I do not actually recall her speaking to me, I recall her playing with me. Mireille was a gifted artist and she was creating a *Little Prince* themed nursery for her baby. I remember that she gave me pieces of felt and that I created alongside her. I remember being in awe of her talent and feeling a sense of warmth and comfort when I was around her. Mireille, somehow, made me feel special, creative and wonderful. Tragically Mireille died in childbirth a few months later. I barely remember her, but her influence on my feelings and abilities encountering new languages has stayed with me to this day.

Twenty years later, I moved to Morocco to teach English. After only a couple of weeks in the country, I suddenly understood and could speak French. I made plenty of mistakes in speaking, but my understanding and pronunciation of the language was very good. I had no idea why. I remember my colleagues asking me how I could speak French when I never had studied it. I couldn't explain it at first, but then I kept having flashbacks of Mireille. Her language had stayed with me all of those years, trapped somewhere in my brain and just waiting to come out. I now feel that the creativity, imagination and love she delivered with her language was important to my retention, and the way she always responded with wonderment at my creations inspired me to keep being creative and taking risks with language. It also continues to inspire me to integrate creative and artistic projects in my teaching and to respond with wonderment when my learners share the wonders of their creativity with me.

Techniques for the Classroom

1. **Give learners multiple ways of showing what they know**: We can give our learners the ability to show what they know in multiple ways. In the field of education these ways are referred to as, 'alternative' or 'authentic' assessments. They include performance assessment, where learners 'perform' or show their knowledge. This can be through an oral or visual presentation, a creative display of knowledge such as a song or a chant, or any other form of transmitting their knowledge that is not bound by the traditional pen and paper format. Portfolio assessment also allows us to see a learner's growth over time. This is not to say that there is no use for traditional testing in the language classroom, but a traditional assessment should be only one of the many different types of assessment you do in a LAF environment.

2. **Give learners time to be creative**: It is necessary to build time into our teaching and learning day for creativity, and especially necessary to give our language learners the extra time they need when using the target language. If everything we do is rushed on a tight schedule, we do not get the chance to think creatively and critically. Sometimes we may tend to think of time that is spent just thinking as wasted, but this time is essential for creativity and imagination to flourish and for language learners to gain the confidence they need in expressing their ideas in the target language.

3. **Use all kinds of materials**: A great benefit of LAF activities that inspire Responding with Wonderment and Awe is that the world around us becomes an important source of materials. Everyday objects become realia, and nature becomes a teaching resource. Teachers can bring things from their own homes, or ask their learners to do the same. The learning materials available in the world around us are endless if we know how to look for them, and having learners that bring a variety of cultural perspectives to the classroom increases the wonderment and awe we might feel from using the diverse materials they share.

4. **Be a creative teacher**: When encouraging language learners to be creative, we must also be creative teachers. We need to be eclectic in our teaching, using different activities, materials and techniques on a regular basis. It is easy for a teacher to fall into a rut. In fact, it is easier to be an ineffective teacher than a good one, but it is also much more likely to lead to bored learners and burned out teachers. Nothing is worse than looking out at a class full of bored students. Do yourself and your learners a favor by tapping into your inner artist, inventor, scientist and responsible risk taker. Learning from you will be something to look forward to, and your relationship with your learners will be closer.

LAF in Class: Creativity, Imagination and Innovation; Responding with Wonderment and Awe

1. Something In My Pocket

Focus On	Speaking, listening
Language Functions Practiced	Describing, explaining, hypothesizing, recounting
Grammar/Vocabulary Practiced	Adjectives, present continuous, modals Vocabulary will depend on what you pull out of your 'pocket'; be certain that most of your learners are familiar with the name of what you will pull out of your pocket and use body language and gestures to provide context.
Grouping Strategy	Individual, whole group
LAF Aspects	• Personal and meaningful: Learners decide what to pull out of their own pockets. • Engaging: Learners are actively engaged in using language to guess. • Uses visuals: In this activity the visuals consist of the body language used by the teachers and learners. • Interactive: Learners interact with one another as speakers and listeners. • Cooperative: Learners cooperate by taking turns pulling something out of their pockets. • Repetition: There is natural repetition as they guess and describe their actions. • Higher order thinking: Learners have to imagine what is being pulled out of a pocket. • Values diversity: Learners get to choose what to pull out of their pockets and can bring in objects from their own culture.
Primary HoM Practiced	Creating, Imagining, and Innovating; Responding with Wonderment and Awe; Communicating with Clarity and Precision; Thinking Flexibly.
Materials Needed	None required, but it is a good idea to know ahead of time what vocabulary you will want to review with your learners. Use vocabulary from readings, dialogues, or other that you have used in the classroom.

STEPS

- Begin with the teacher pretending to pull something out of his or her pocket.
- The imaginary object is then 'used' in the way that it would traditionally be used.
- Body language, gestures and movements are all clues to what the object is.
- For example, you can pretend that you are pulling a mirror out of your pocket and pretend to hold it up and look at yourself in it, fixing your hair and making faces so that the learners can guess what you pulled out of your pocket. In the meantime, you are using language to assist you by saying something like, "Oh, I'm having a terrible hair day!"
- The activity proceeds with learners guessing what the object is, either by taking turns or shouting out what has been pulled out of the pocket.
- It becomes more fun and more challenging as more and more unlikely things are pulled out of the pocket, such as an elephant or a motorboat.
- Extend the activity by having learners take turns pulling things out of their pockets as well while other learners guess the object.
- The activity may be done purely with the imagination or you can provide vocabulary cards or pictures to choose from.
- The use of vocabulary cards or pictures can help to incorporate the specific content you are learning while also promoting the use of creativity in 'using' an object without naming it.
- To make the activity truly challenging it is a nice idea to switch between concrete objects to feelings or abstract concepts.

Adaptations	Make it easier by modeling more, using more gestures and body language, and pulling out concrete objects that the learners are familiar with. Make it harder by limiting the use of gestures and body language and putting abstract concepts out of your pocket, or by having learners pull whatever they want out of their pockets without the use of gestures or body language. Also, imposing a time limit will add to the challenge.
Remote Learning	This activity can easily be adapted to remote learning without any special modifications as long as the learners are able to see and hear one another.

2. Invent-A-Gadget

Focus On	Speaking and listening with a writing extension
Language Functions	Agreeing, disagreeing, giving directions, giving opinions, contradicting, supporting
Grammar/ Vocabulary Practice	Declaratives, prepositions, adjectives Vocabulary depends on your specific gadget and materials but will include words for giving directions and adjectives.
Grouping Strategy	Small groups or pairs
LAF Aspects	<ul><li>Personal and meaningful: Learners decide what to create using their own materials or those they choose.</li><li>Engaging: Learners are actively engaged in completing the task while using language.</li><li>Uses visuals: In this activity the visuals consist of the materials used.</li><li>Interactive: Learners interact with one another as speakers and listeners.</li><li>Cooperative: Learners cooperate in small groups.</li><li>Purposeful: Learners create a new product.</li><li>Repetition: There is natural repetition as they decide what to create and how.</li><li>Higher order thinking: Learners have to imagine and innovate in order to create a new product.</li><li>Values diversity: Learners get to choose what to create and can rely on their own background experiences.</li></ul>
Materials Needed	Recyclable materials, trash, or any object that is no longer wanted or needed. Have learners bring objects from home as well. You will also use tape, glue, scissors and markers.

STEPS

- Collect recyclable materials, trash or anything unwanted and ask learners to contribute their own.
- Once you have plenty of options, separate items into paper grocery bags with at least 10 objects in each bag. Seal the bags.
- Have learners work in small cooperative groups.
- Give each group a sealed grocery bag with 10 items and explain that they have only the items in the bag to create a new gadget an adult would find useful, or a toy that a child would want to play with.
- Provide additional resources of tape, glue, scissors and a marker to use, but those are the only additional resources they have.
- Make sure that before they begin to create their new invention they plan out what they will be doing and create a design for their new gadget or toy on a sheet of paper.
- Give students enough time to create their new gadget or toy and to come up with a sales pitch or commercial for their new invention.
- Record the presentations, if possible ,to watch as a class and vote on the best gadget or toy.

Adaptations	<u>Make it easier</u> by giving learners a form for planning their new invention with categories they can fill in. Also demonstrate with your own invention, or one you find online made from found objects, and show a sales pitch or commercial for a new product as a guide. <u>Make it harder</u> by giving learners less modeling and direction and imposing a tighter time limit on them. Further the language use needed by having them create a one-minute commercial for their product with a written script that ensures that each person in the group participates.
Remote Learning	This activity is difficult to adapt to remote learning if learners are not together. However, it can become an individual activity that learners do for homework with found objects in their home and they can present to one another remotely.

3. Are you kidding me?

Language Skill Focus	Speaking, listening
Language Functions Practiced	Asking and answering questions, making comparisons, complaining, explaining, denying, expressing preferences, persuading, making demands, expressing empathy
Grammar/Vocabulary Practiced	Interrogatives, comparatives, past and present tense Vocabulary will depend on the role plays; a word bank can be provided along with role play topics to support learners.
Grouping Strategy	Pairs, whole group
LAF Aspects	<ul><li>Personal and meaningful: Learners give their own opinions and thoughts using their own language skills, not a script.</li><li>Engaging: Learners generally enjoy talking about things that are meaningful to them.</li><li>Interactive: There is no way to do this without interacting.</li><li>Cooperative: They must listen and cooperate to complete the activity.</li><li>Values diversity: Different perspectives are allowed and welcomed.</li><li>Higher order thinking: Learners must think abstractly to respond.</li><li>Task based: There is a specific task that learners must accomplish.</li></ul>
Primary HoM Practiced	Responding with Wonderment and Awe; Creating, Imagining and Innovating; Listening with Understanding and Empathy; Thinking Interdependently; Thinking Flexibly
Materials Needed	None are necessary, but props and realia could help.

STEPS

- Separate learners into pairs or small groups.
- Have them create role plays where one member of the pair is proposing an outrageous, amazing or shocking idea to the other. They can create their own scenarios or you can offer scenarios to them.
- The situations will depend on the age of the learners, their environment, and interests, but could include the following: running for president, sailing around the world, getting married without ever meeting your partner beforehand, robbing a bank, playing a prank on the principal, eating a bag full of spiders, etc.
- Have learners use their imaginations to determine how to respond to the prompt and role play their responses.
- Give lower level language learners more modeling, short readings or short unfinished dialogues to inspire the role play, sentences starters, and a word and phrase bank to pull from.

Sentence Starters	Word/Phrase Bank
"Why did you ….?"	"Really?"
"Why would you ever,…?"	"You know what I mean?"
"When are you going to….?"	"I don't get it."
"Listen, I want to tell you…"	"Are you out of your mind?"

- Serve as a guide and facilitator for the most part, rather than the director of the role play. When learners are their own directors, they are employing many Habits of Mind as critical, creative thinkers and problem solvers.
- You can further your lesson with characters or topics from readings and books.

Adaptations	<u>Make it easier</u>: Give lower level language learners more modeling, short readings or short unfinished dialogues to inspire the role play. You can provide sentences starters and a word and phrase bank to pull from. You can also cut down on the time each person is expected to speak. <u>Make it harder:</u> Give each speaker more time to elaborate on the topic so they have to fill that time with language, giving topics that are more challenging to talk about.
Remote Learning	It is more difficult to do role plays using remote learning, but not impossible. If you can, put learners in pairs in separate virtual rooms after they have seen the modeling and received the scaffolds they need to work on their role plays. Then be sure to visit rooms for support and guidance while they are working. Give them enough time to work together before presenting their role plays to the whole group back in your online classroom.

4. Franken-Animals

Language Skill Focus	Listening and speaking with writing extension
Language Functions Practiced	Describing, giving opinions, pondering, suggesting
Grammar/Vocabulary Practiced	Modals, conditionals Vocabulary depends on animals created; includes adjectives.
Grouping Strategy	Individual, pairs, whole group
LAF Aspects	• Personal and meaningful: Learners are creating something of their own. • Engaging: Learners are actively engaged in drawing. • Uses visuals: Learners create their own visuals. • Interactive: Learners interact with one another to complete the task. • Cooperative: Learners cooperate in pairs to complete the activity. • Purposeful: Learners invent a whole new animal and create a backstory for that animal. • Repetition: There is repetition and restating as they decide how to describe their new creations. • Higher order thinking: Learners have to come up with a whole new animal, habitat, etc. • Values diversity: Different ways of seeing the world are inherent in the activity.
Primary HoM Practiced	Thinking Flexibly, Thinking Interdependently, Finding Humor
Materials Needed	Large pieces of paper and markers, crayons, colored pencils or any other device to draw with.

STEPS

- Brainstorm different kinds of animals that are found in different habitats and locations with your learners. For example, at a zoo, farm, ocean, jungle, etc.
- Create a semantic web so that learners have a visual of the kinds of animals that are found in different places as well as a bank of words to choose from.
- Ask volunteers to give short descriptions of their favorite animals and have others guess what that animal is.
- Ask volunteers to compare and contrast two animals without naming them and have the rest of the class guess those two animals.
- Give each learner a sheet of paper and explain that they will be doing an activity together.
- Depending on the age and language level of your learners, you might want to recall prior knowledge for them and see if they are aware of the Frankenstein story. Show a visual if possible and gather from them what they know about this tale. Tell them that they will be creating a new creature like Dr. Frankenstein did with the activity they are about to do.
- Arrange learners in back-to-back pairs and have each learner fold their paper in half vertically; make sure that you are modeling this for your learners.
- Tell each learner that on one side of their folded paper they will draw the head and neck of any animal they choose to draw and model by drawing the head and neck of any animal. They are not to reveal this to their partner.
- Show them how to extend the neck of the animal they draw a small amount on the opposite side of the fold so that when the paper is folded, only two neck lines can be seen representing the neck of the animal that was drawn on the opposite side of the paper.
- Have partners exchange papers showing only the side with a small segment of neck drawn. Make sure to emphasize that there is no flipping over of the paper to see the animal head that was drawn.
- Have partners draw the **body** of any animal they would like to draw on the paper they received.
- Encourage learners to be as detailed as they can with their drawing.
- Give a time limit here or it can go on forever. I suggest three to five minutes.
- Exchange the papers again and have partners open their folded papers flat to see a whole new animal.
- This should be quite amusing because the body that one person drew rarely goes with the head of the original drawing.
- Tell learners that they have created a new species of animal.
- Have learner pairs work together to name their new animals, give them a habitat, and list some facts about the animal, including what it eats, how it spends its days, and other interesting facts that they will present to the class.
- An activity extension can be to write a short paragraph, poem or song about the new species of animal.

Adaptations	<u>Make it easier:</u> Give learners more modeling and examples before you begin. Keep a word bank on the board of animals and adjectives to describe them, or make sure your semantic web contains a lot of useful vocabulary for the second part of the activity <u>Make it harder:</u> Encourage learners to draw animals that are not commonly found or known. You can increase the demands by having learners write a short story together about their animal or joining pairs to role play how their animals might interact if they could speak to one another.
Remote Learning	This activity can be adapted to remote learning with some creative thinking. You can ask half of your learners to draw on their own papers a head and neck of an animal, and the other half a neck and body. Then pair up a head learner with a body learner in break out rooms and have them put their drawings together virtually. This can be done by either having one learner redraw the anumal or by using actual software to put the drawings together, such as Photoshop or Picstitch. After that the activity can proceed as in the actual classroom.

5. Five in Five

Language Skill Focus	Writing, reading with speaking and listening extension
Language Functions Practiced	Predicting, describing, explaining, justifying
Grammar/Vocabulary Practiced	Future tense, modals, conditionals Vocabulary depends on what learners choose to imagine for themselves.
Grouping Strategy	Individual, pairs, whole group
LAF Aspects	<ul><li>Personal and meaningful: Learners are talking about their own futures.</li><li>Engaging: Learners are actively engaged in predicting.</li><li>Uses visuals: Learners create their own visuals.</li><li>Interactive: Learners interact with one another to complete the task.</li><li>Cooperative: Learners cooperate to complete the activity.</li><li>Repetition: There is repetition and restating as they decide on how to create their updates.</li><li>Higher order thinking: Learners have to come up with ideas on their own.</li><li>Values diversity: Different ways of seeing the world are inherent in the activity.</li></ul>
Primary HoM Practiced	Creating, Imagining and Innovating, Thinking Flexibly, Thinking Interdependently, Applying Past Knowledge to New Situations
Materials Needed	Paper and writing instruments for learners

STEPS

- Tell students you will be doing an activity that imagines life five years from now.
- Brainstorm with the class what kinds of changes will take place in the world, in the country, and in the community five years from now. Write their ideas on the board.
- Next, tell them to imagine how their own lives will be in five years. Model this by imagining your life five years from now and coming up with five things you think will be happening in your own life. Write these things on the board, pointing out your use of the following:

  a. Simple future tense. (Eg., I will live in Maine. I will be an artist.)
  b. Modals. (Eg., I might have a horse. I could have a new baby.)
  c. Conditionals (Eg., If I write a book, I will go on a book tour.)

- Review the grammar needed to complete the activity with learners.
- Next, give learners time to write their own five life updates for five years from now. As learners are writing, circulate and answer any grammar questions or provide any vocabulary they need.
- Once learners are finished, ask them to choose a symbol to represent their lives in five years and add that to their paper. Give examples of symbols such as a heart, etc. Learners should NOT put their names on their papers.
- Collect papers and redistribute to the class so no learner ends up with his or her own paper.
- Ask learners to read what their classmate has written and think about who that classmate might be.
- Take turns having learners read the paper they have out loud and describe the symbol on the paper to the whole class (without showing it). Then have learner take three guesses as to who wrote the paper they have.
- As an extension, conduct a whole class activity on the imagined futures and create a semantic web or chart on the board showing the similarities and differences among learners.

Adaptations	<u>Make it easier:</u> Give learners more modeling and examples before you begin. Pair up learners to help one another with their future imaginings. <u>Make it harder:</u> Give learners less time to come up with their five ideas for the future and/or give limitations on what they can imagine or the vocabulary or grammar they can use.
Remote Learning	This activity can easily be adapted to remote learning without any need for changes.

Chapter 12
LAF with Applying Past Knowledge to New Situations and Learning Continuously

As teachers, we bring our own experiences and knowledge to the classroom, and so do our language learners. No matter their ages or language levels, all learners come with a host of background experiences and memories that are essential to who they are. These experiences can and should be integrated into classroom activities whenever possible. By validating and incorporating their personal journeys in the language classroom, you are making your activities personal and meaningful (LAF) and being a culturally responsive educator.

True Stories of TESOL

I always say that I learn as much from my learners as they do from me. They come to the classroom with such a diverse set of experiences and backgrounds that our class is always enriched by their knowledge. Many times language learners have taught me how to be a better teacher by the way they respond to my activities. They have also taught me that it is important to always keep an open mind and a flexible spirit in the language classroom.

When I was a young teacher in Costa Rica, I was privileged to work with a group of very enthusiastic learners. One of my groups came to my class every day after their cross-cultural activity. They were working with a wonderful cross-cultural trainer from the School for International Training in Vermont. She came to Costa Rica with a whole host of active and participatory cross-cultural training activities to do with the learners, and the learners enjoyed every minute of them. I soon got into the daily habit of asking my learners what they had learned during cross-cultural training. Since they enjoyed the training so much, they were always eager to teach me the activities.

I played a bit of a trick on my Costa Rican students that year. I did not tell them that I spoke Spanish until the very last day of class. Because of this, they thought that they had to teach me the cross-cultural training activity in English. I admit that sometimes I acted as though I did not understand things that were clear to me, just to get them to use their body language and all of the discourse strategies I had taught them.

By the end of the semester I had learned a great deal of wonderful cross-cultural training activities that I turned into LAF activities for future classes by adapting them and including a language focus. At the same time, my students gained valuable practice in communicating important concepts in English. I am not even sure who learned more, them or me. It was definitely a win-win situation. I still use those activities to this day, and I know that my students felt empowered and were able to practice a great deal of language in their role as 'teachers' while reinforcing the cross-cultural training for themselves.

Techniques in the Classroom

In order to remember to keep learning from my learners, and to encourage learners to apply the knowledge they bring to the classroom, I made up the acronym LEARN. If I am ever feeling a bit uncertain of the climate in my classroom, I try to remember to keep these things in mind.

1. **L - Let learners be teachers.** When learners are empowered to teach something, they immediately take more risks and interact more in the target language. In addition, temporarily becoming an expert in the classroom on a certain subject can give learners a boost of confidence and the self-esteem they need to continue learning a language and culture that differs from their own.

2. **E – Encourage learners to continue learning outside the classroom.** No matter how wonderfully creative, innovative and engaging your lessons are, learners need more time interacting in and being exposed to the target language outside of the classroom.

3. **A – Acknowledge what learners bring with them to the classroom.** Every second language learner necessarily has a first language and culture they come from. For many of them, this native language and culture can help them to understand the new language and culture in many ways.

4. **R – Remind learners that language learning never ends.** Sometimes learners are impatient to learn everything they need to know in a language. However, we are never done learning new vocabulary and new ways of communicating. Remind learners that even you learn new words every year, and encourage them to bring new words and phrases to class to teach everyone else.

5. **N – Notice what learners are struggling with.** A part of learning continuously as a teacher is being in tune with each new group of learners. Sometimes the same mistakes or challenges will appear during every class, and language learners will struggle with certain forms or concepts. Make sure that you take the time to acknowledge this and provide focused practice and discussion for language your learners find most challenging.

LAF in Class:
Learning Continuously and Applying Past Knowledge to New Situations

1. Thinking Journey

Language Skill Focus	Listening, speaking
Language Functions Practiced	Describing, giving opinions, pondering, giving and following directions
Grammar/Vocabulary Practiced	Simple present, simple past, past continuous. Vocabulary depends on learners' thoughts.
Grouping Strategy	Individual, small group, whole group
LAF Aspects	• Personal and meaningful: Learners are talking about themselves. • Engaging: They are finding out about one another and reminiscing about their own lives. • Uses visuals: Old photographs can be used. • Interactive: Learners interact with one another to complete the task. • Cooperative: They must cooperate in small groups to complete the activity. • Purposeful: Learners are expressing their own thinking journeys by completing the task and teaching others about themselves. • Repetition: There is repetition and restating as they describe. • Higher order thinking: Learners have to come up with ideas about how they have changed over time. • Values diversity: Different ways of seeing the world and oneself are part of the activity.
Primary HoM Practiced	Thinking Flexibly, Thinking Interdependently, Creating, Imagining and Innovating
Materials Needed	No materials are needed for this activity except for the learners themselves, but I would recommend a journal for recording reflections after the activity is over.

STEPS

- Ask learners to close their eyes and visualize themselves five years ago (With kids ages 6-10 you might have to say two years ago).

- Ask them to remember what they looked like, what they enjoyed doing, who their friends were, or anything they can remember from that time.

- For modeling, you can bring in and show an old photo album. You can also ask learners to bring these to class ahead of time if they have videos or photos of themselves from the past.

- If learners have brought their own photos, ask them to share in small groups or with the whole class without comment, just showing. This serves to generate interest.

- Next, ask learners the following question, using the "I used to think…, now I think…" visible thinking routine: "What did you used to think was true or important X years ago, that now you feel differently about? This could be something in your personal or academic life. Think about how you have grown and changed and how you think differently now based on your experiences or maybe things you have learned."

- You may model with your own response to this question if needed, starting with, "I used to think….and now I think…."

- Give learners a few minutes to formulate their thoughts on this. Remember, language learners will almost always need more time than native speakers to gather their thoughts and be able to express them in the target language.

- Put learners in small cooperative groups of two to four people to share their thoughts.

- Provide enough time for each learner to share. Explain that they will be sharing with the whole group, and that they will need to remember what their partners have said.

- Put learners back in a whole group setting and ask them to share one of their cooperative group partner's thoughts.

- Note: If you ask learners to share their own thoughts then they don't really have to listen to their partners, and they do not get the language practice of not only expressing their own thoughts but also summarizing and recounting the words of another person. This provides additional language practice.

Examples from Language Learners

1. *"Roberto said he used to think that English will be easy but now he thinks it not so easy!"*
2. *"Alejandra is used to think that she will never like peanut butter but now she like it!"*

Notice that in both of these examples learners have brought up conditions that stemmed from their immigration and linguistic/cultural journey. Notice also that both examples have errors. After each of these I would repeat by modeling the correct usage.

1. *"So, Roberto used to think that learning would be easy, but now he thinks it's not so easy?"*
2. *"So, Alejandra used to think that she could never like peanut butter but now she likes it?"*

This modeling with the correct form allows learners to hear the standard way of expressing their thoughts in English. Some learners will pick up on the correction and repeat it, thereby self-correcting, and others might not. Some will stop me and question their grammar. By forming my modeling/correction as a question, I am giving them an additional opportunity to respond in English and thus practice the target language.

Adaptations	<u>Make it easier:</u> Give learners several of your own examples and modeling before asking them to contribute their own ideas. You may use images that demonstrate how you have changed over time. Provide words that they can use on the board and sentence stems. <u>Make it harder:</u> Give learners less modeling and less time to gather their thoughts. Give them categories that they have to adhere to in their answers. For example, their answers have to be about science or about government, etc.
Remote Learning	This activity is easily adapted to remote learning. You can display an image and go about the same steps you would in a face-to -ace classroom. Students can be placed in small groups in virtual rooms and you as the teacher can visit the rooms to provide help and guidance as needed to lower level learners.

2. What would you do?

Focus On	Reading, listening and speaking with writing extension
Language Functions Practiced	Explaining, describing, making propositions, making excuses
Grammar/Vocabulary Practiced	Simple past, past continuous, present perfect, modals; vocabulary depends on topics chosen
Grouping Strategy	Pairs and whole group, individual extensions
LAF Aspects	• Personal and meaningful: Learners give their own opinions and ideas. • Engaging: Learners generally enjoy this activity because it highlights differences of opinion. • Interactive: There is no way to do this without interacting. • Cooperative: They must cooperate in pairs to complete the activity. • Purposeful: Learners are grappling with issues beyond language. • Repetition: There is natural repetition during this activity. • Higher order thinking: Learners must think of how they would react in different situations. • Values Diversity: A variety of perspectives and possibilities are welcome and encouraged.
Primary HoM Practiced	Applying Past Knowledge to New Situations; Learning Continuously; Managing Impulsivity; Persisting; Listening with Understanding and Empathy; Thinking Interdependently; Thinking Flexibly
Materials Needed	Stories, history lessons, reports or readings about the negative consequences of being impulsive, or of not being persistent. There are a number of websites that feature these accounts for young learners (for accounts involving peer pressure see https://yourlifecounts.org). Another option is to create stories on your own. You should have a minimum of two short stories or accounts about a paragraph long for each pair of learners in your class. It is okay to use the same two stories for some pairs, but try to have as much variety as possible.

STEPS

- Put language learners in pairs and give each pair one account of someone making a difficult choice or decision.
- Have one member of the pair read the account to the other member of the pair.
- Encourage questioning for clarification and understanding.
- Have pairs brainstorm what they would do if they were in similar circumstances. Encourage them to use their imaginations to come up with strategies and ideas for dealing with the situation they have read about and discussed.
- Have pairs create written accounts or dialogues of how the situation might have been handled differently, or create their own scenarios with a similar situation and a different choice. Some sample scenarios are included below.
- Have pairs present to the class.

Possible Scenarios

All of your friends are going to a concert and want you to join them. You know that if you buy a ticket to the concert you will not have enough money for the things you need. What would you do?
You see a young woman in a grocery store steal food by putting it in her bag. She is with two small children. What would you do?
You see a father yelling at his young son in a store. He is yanking the child by the arm and telling him he is a loser. What would you do?
You see your best friend's fiancée holding hands with someone else in a restaurant. You are meeting your best friend right after you see this. What would you do?

Adaptations	Make it easier: Provide plenty of context by giving learners visual representations of the readings. Be sure that the readings are at their level or slightly higher and do frequent comprehension checks. Make it harder: Provide scenarios for students that are written at a higher level. Give them less time to think about them and/or have them come up with their own scenarios to write and give to one another.
Remote Learning	This activity is easily adapted to remote learning by giving your learners the scenarios to read before the class. Once students are together, be sure to do comprehension checks and then continue with your discussion. You can separate students in virtual rooms in pairs to come up with their own scenarios to share with the whole class.

3. Pet Peeves

Language Skill Focus	Listening, speaking
Language Functions Practiced	Explaining, describing, asking and answering questions
Grammar/Vocabulary Practiced	Simple past, past continuous; vocabulary depends on topics chosen
Grouping Strategy	Pairs and whole group, individual extensions
LAF Aspects	<ul><li>Personal and meaningful: Learners get to talk about themselves and what is important to them.</li><li>Engaging: Learners generally enjoy this activity because it involves getting to know peers better.</li><li>Interactive: Learners interact with one another as well as with the teacher.</li><li>Cooperative: This activity uses the cooperative learning structure: think, write, pair, share (TWPS).</li><li>Repetition: There is natural repetition during this activity.</li><li>Purposeful: Learners are teaching others something important about themselves.</li><li>Higher order thinking: Learners must think of critically about their own triggers and ponder why they exist.</li><li>Values diversity: A variety of perspectives and possibilities are a natural consequence of this activity.</li></ul>
Primary HoM Practiced	Applying Past Knowledge to New Situations; Learning Continuously; Persisting; Listening with Understanding and Empathy; Thinking Interdependently; Thinking Flexibly
Materials Needed	If possible, provide beanbags or balls and yoga mats or comfortable pillows to sit on.

STEPS

- Explain the concept of 'pet peeves' to your language learners and give them an example of a pet peeve you have.
- Tell them they will be doing a Think, Write, Pair, Share (TWPS) to explain and talk about one of their own pet peeves.
- First give your learners at least one minute to THINK about their pet peeve without writing anything down.
- Next, give them two to three minutes to write about their pet peeve.
- Next, pair up learners and have them exchange papers, read one another's papers, and talk about them together for five to 10 minutes.
- Finally, have pairs share what they learned about one another with the whole group.
- During the sharing part of the activity you might create a semantic web on the board to show what the pet peeves are in the class and to find any categories or similarities among learners.
- An example of a pet peeve might be lateness. Since there are different cultural perceptions of time and punctuality, this type of pet peeve can open a window into multiple perspectives and diverse ways of knowing. What is an acceptable amount of lateness in one culture can be considered extremely rude in another. People from the punctual culture may respond negatively to people from another culture that has a more flexible idea of time.

Adaptations	Make it easier: Provide plenty of context and scaffolding by using visuals and body language to explain the pet peeves. Provide a word or phrase bank as needed Make it harder: Provide less modeling and/or give examples that are more complex and rely heavily on language to be understood.
Remote Learning	This activity is easily adapted to remote learning by providing students with the modeling and directions, then completing the TWPS by separating learners in paired remote rooms, and later bringing them back together to the whole group.

4. You are the Expert

Focus On	Listening, speaking, reading and writing
Language Functions Practiced	Explaining, describing, asking and answering questions, following directions, giving directions
Grammar/Vocabulary Practiced	Commands, declaratives, simple present, simple past, past continuous; vocabulary depends on topics chosen
Grouping Strategy	Pairs and whole group, individual extensions
LAF Aspects	<ul><li>Personal and meaningful: Learners get to teach something they have expertise in.</li><li>Engaging: Learners generally enjoy this activity because it involves learning something new.</li><li>Interactive: Learners interact with one another as well as with the teacher.</li><li>Cooperative: They must cooperate in pairs to complete the activity.</li><li>Repetition: There is natural repetition during this activity.</li><li>Purposeful: Learners are teaching a specific skill to the class.</li><li>Higher order thinking: Learners must think critically in order to explain their area of expertise and learn that of their partner.</li><li>Values diversity: A variety of perspectives and possibilities are a natural consequence of this activity.</li><li>Task-based: Learners are engaged in completing a specific task.</li></ul>
Primary HoM Practiced	Learning Continuously, Persisting, Communicating with Clarity and Precision, Striving for Accuracy Thinking Interdependently
Materials Needed	No materials are necessary, but for the extension activity learners can bring in props or materials to teach the rest of the class their area of expertise.

STEPS

- Write the word 'expert' on the board and ask learners to brainstorm what that means. Write down their ideas in a semantic web, and solicit and include examples of well-known or famous experts.
- Tell learners that everyone is an expert at something. Give an example of what you are an expert on. For example, cooking a certain dish, decorating for parties, playing an instrument, parenting your child, reading mysteries, or whatever else you feel like an 'expert' doing.
- Ask students to think about something they are experts in and to free write about that for about three minutes, but not to share their paper or their area of expertise with anyone. It is a secret!
- Have learners prepare a one-minute 'lesson' on their area of expertise with the following criteria: Without naming it, and without using body language, learners talk about their area of expertise. They can mention when they do this thing, what it means to them, how they learned it, etc.
- Once learners have finished, the rest of the class gets three guesses to find out what they are experts in. If nobody guesses correctly, the learner continues to talk about his or her area of expertise for fifteen seconds. This continues until somebody guesses the area.
- If there are still no correct guesses, ask learners to use some body language to help the class.
- As an extension, learners can work in small groups to teach an area of expertise to the rest of the class. This works well if there are several learners with the same or similar expertise from a certain cultural group. For example, expertise in a certain dance, food preparation, calligraphy, etc.

Adaptations	<u>Make it easier</u>: Provide plenty of modeling for learners by having them guess several of your areas of expertise first. Generate vocabulary with learners that they might need to describe their areas. <u>Make it harder</u>: Do not provide modeling for learners and increase the challenge by limiting the kinds of things that they are allowed to say about their area of expertise. For example, they might not be able to say anything about when they do this or how it is done, only talk around the topic.
Remote Learning	This activity is easily adapted to remote learning without any need to change the sequence of events.

5. Find Someone Who…the LAF way

Focus On	Listening, speaking and writing
Language Functions Practiced	Asking and answering questions, explaining, describing, following directions, giving directions
Grammar/Vocabulary Practiced	Interrogatives, past tense, present tense, declaratives, simple present, simple past, past continuous Vocabulary depends on the categories you choose.
Grouping Strategy	Pairs and whole group, individual extensions
LAF Aspects	<ul><li>Personal and meaningful: Learners get to talk about themselves.</li><li>Engaging: Learners generally enjoy this activity because it involves learning something new and moving around.</li><li>Interactive: Learners interact with one another as well as with the teacher.</li><li>Cooperative: They must cooperate to complete the activity.</li><li>Purposeful: The chart must be filled in at the end of the activity.</li><li>Repetition: There is natural repetition during this activity.</li><li>Higher order thinking: Learners must think critically in order to respond to the 'why' questions.</li><li>Values diversity: A variety of perspectives and possibilities are a natural consequence of this activity.</li></ul>
Primary HoM Practiced	Learning Continuously, Applying Past Knowledge to New Situations, Communicating with Clarity and Precision, Striving for Accuracy, Thinking Interdependently
Materials Needed	"Find Someone Who…" chart below, or create a new one on your own.

STEPS

- Give each learner a copy of the chart below, or make your own chart.
- Have learners mingle and talk to discover who belongs in each square.
- Learners can only put their own names in one of the squares. Every other square has to have a classmate's name and response to the follow-up question.
- In addition to finding out who belongs in each square and getting their names, learners need to ask follow-up questions with the question word found in the square.
- Encourage learners to try to get a different name for each square so they talk to as many other learners as possible.
- As an alternative, let learners loose in a situation where they can mingle with individuals outside of the class for a variety of answers and perspectives.

Below is one chart, but feel free to create your own with what you have learned about your learners and the kinds of language and topics you want them to explore.

Is very persistent. How?	Does not enjoy movies. Why?	Can tell a funny joke. What?	Can play a musical instrument well. Which one?
Has lost his or her temper recently. How?	Has vacationed on an island. Where?	Has run in a marathon. When?	Loves to cook. What?
Can do an imitation of a celebrity. Who?	Has seen a ghost. Where?	Can do a magic trick. How?	Has been to more than three countries. Where?
Has a strange relative. Who?	Is good at a sport. Which one?	Gave up on something he/she wanted to do. Why?	Can recite a poem from memory. Which one?

Adaptations	<u>Make it easier:</u> – Complete the activity as a whole class first, with a demonstration topic and follow-up question. Have learners mingle in pairs rather than individually. <u>Make it harder:</u> Increase the challenge by imposing a time limit and including harder categories and follow-up question types in your chart. Another option is to have several different charts for different learners so there is more variety in the questions asked.
Remote Learning	This activity is easily adapted to remote learning without any need to change the sequence of events.

Chapter 13
Conclusion: Keep on LAF-ing with all of the Habits of Mind

I hope you are able to use many of the activities in this book and that you have learned the skills to create many others. Every teacher has their own unique way of teaching and their own unique challenges. If you come across some ideas in this book that simply do not work for your teaching situation, feel free to discard them or adapt them to make them work for you. I have found in my teaching that my best lessons are built around ideas that I have gathered from other instructors and changed to suit my own way of teaching. Often those ideas will remind me of something I learned in graduate school or read about somewhere. It will prompt me to look back on written resources to understand why a certain teaching/learning activity appeals to me. Rarely do I come up with something by pulling it out of thin air. I use my past experiences, my creativity and my flexibility to change things up and rework them to meet my learners' needs, as well as my own. In other words, I use my Habits of Mind, and I hope you will as well.

The following are some useful questions to ask yourself as you develop your own activities based on the LAF list of what works for promoting second language acquisition.

Questions To Ask Yourself:
- Is the activity **engaging**? Will it be fun for the learner and the teacher? Making an activity as engaging as possible is important, as that will increase the motivation and the excitement about learning. Habits of Mind connection: Finding Humor, Responding with Wonderment and Awe, Creating, Imagining and Innovating, Taking Responsible Risks.
- Is the activity **interactive**? Will the student need to interact in some way using language to complete the activity? Making an activity interactive ensures that learners are practicing what they need to achieve communicative competence. Habits of Mind connection: Thinking Interdependently, Communicating with Clarity and Precision, Questioning and Problem Posing, Striving for Accuracy.
- Is the activity **cooperative**? Does the learner need another learner or learners to complete the activity? Making an activity cooperative so that everyone has an important role to play is an assurance that language will be used by all learners and nobody will be left out. Habits of Mind connection: Thinking Interdependently, Striving for Accuracy, Questioning and Problem Posing, Communicating with Clarity and Precision, Managing Impulsivity, Persisting, Learning Continuously, Applying Past Knowledge to New Situations.
- Does the activity **value diversity**? Are multiple perspectives allowed and encouraged? When more than one viewpoint or perspective is allowed and valued in the language classroom, culturally responsive pedagogy is encouraged and the classroom becomes a more welcoming place. Habits of Mind connection: Metacognition, Thinking Flexibly, Listening with Empathy and Understanding, Learning Continuously, Applying Past Knowledge to New Situations, Responding with Wonderment and Awe.

- Does the activity promote **higher order thinking**? Does it call for being a creative and critical thinker? This is probably the most important consideration when learning through the Habits of Mind. If an activity is boring or rote, then it probably should be tossed out or better yet, modified. Habits of Mind connection: all of them.

- Is the activity **adaptable**? Can you change it to meet the needs of different learners? This is an important consideration when you are creating an activity or using one you find. If you can recycle the activity to use over and over again and to target different content areas or levels of proficiency, then that is a great activity to have in your repertoire. Habits of Mind connection: Thinking Flexibly, Creating, Imagining and Innovating, Taking Responsible Risks, Persisting.

- Is the activity **personal and meaningful**? Can your learners identify with the activity in a way that allows them to create a connection to the learning? I have found that making activities personal and meaningful greatly enhances the curiosity and the engagement of learners in ways that allow them to relate to the content being studied and to apply new knowledge far beyond the time of the lesson. Habits of Mind connection: Managing Impulsivity, Taking Responsible Risks, Listening with Empathy and Understanding, Applying Past Knowledge to New Situations.

- Have I given **clear directions** and **modeled** how to do the activity for my learners? No matter how great your activity is, if your learners aren't sure what they are supposed to be doing, the activity won't work. One great way to get learners to understand is to model, repeatedly if necessary. Habits of Mind connection: Striving for Accuracy, Communicating with Clarity and Precision.

- Am I **error correcting** in a way that promotes further interactive language practice and empowers learners? There are always multiple opportunities to error correct in the language classroom, but not all of these opportunities should be taken. We want to make sure that we don't interrupt an interaction or inhibit a learner through error correction. Ask yourself if you can wait until the end of class to go over errors, or error correct through modeling and restating within the interaction. Another way is to develop a technique that alerts a learner that an error has been made and give him or her a chance to self-correct. Habits of Mind connection: Listening with Understanding and Empathy, Communicating with Clarity and Precision, Striving for Accuracy, Finding Humor.

Hopefully, the ideas put forth in this book will inspire you and your learners to further explore the Habits of Mind and regularly integrate critical and creative thinking into your teaching and learning. The choice to guide language learners in their pursuit of a new language and culture is a brave choice to make as a teacher. You are undoubtedly practicing the HoM with your learners every time you step into the classroom. It takes plenty of persistence and lots of listening to be able to meet your learners' needs. I hope this book gives you some additional tools to put in your teaching bag as well as the inspiration to become the most creative teacher you can be.

References

Anderson, L.W., Krathwohl, D.R., Airasian, P.W., Cruikshank, K.A., Mayer, R.E., Pintrich, P.R., Raths, J., Wittrock, M.C. (2001). *A Taxonomy for Learning, Teaching, and Assessing: A revision of Bloom's Taxonomy of Educational Objectives*. New York: Pearson, Allyn & Bacon.

Berko Gleason, J. & N. Bernstein-Ratner (eds.) (2009). The Development of Language 7th edn. New York: Allyn and Bacon.

Bialystok, E. (2001). *Bilingualism in Development: Language, literacy, and Cognition*. Cambridge: Cambridge University Press.

Christison, M. & Bassano, S. (1987). Look who's talking!: Photocopiable strategies for developing group interaction. Hayward, CA: Alta Book Center Publishers.

Chomsky, N. (1959). Review of verbal behavior by B.F. Skinner. *Language*, 35/1.26-58.

Collier, V.P. (1989). 'How long? A synthesis of research on academic achievement in a second language.' *TESOL Quarterly* 23/3.509-31.

Cook, V. (2003). 'The poverty of the stimulus argument and structure-dependency in L2 users of English.' *International Review of Applied Linguistics*, 41/3. 201-21.

Costa, A., & Kallick, B. (2000). Describing 16 habits of mind.

Costa, A. L., & Kallick, B. (2008). *Learning and leading with habits of mind: 16 essential characteristics for success*. Alexandria, VA: Association for Supervision and Curriculum Development.

Costa, A. L., & Kallick, B. (2014). *Dispositions: Reframing teaching and learning*. Thousand Oaks, CA: Corwin Press.

Cummins, J. (2000). *Language, Power, and Pedagogy: Bilingual Children in the Crossfire*. Clevedon: Multilingual Matters.

Dörnyei, Z. (2009). The Psychology of Second Language Acquisition. Oxford: Oxford University Press.

Ellis, R. & G. Barkhuizen. (2005). *Analysing Learner Language*. Oxford: Oxford University Press.

Ellis, R. (2012). Language Teaching Research and Language Pedagogy. Malden, M.A.: Wiley-Blackwell.

Gass, S.M. (1997). *Input, Interaction, and the Second Language Learner*. Mahwah, N.J.: Lawrence Erlbaum and Associates.

Gass, S.M. (2010). Interactionist perspectives on second language acquisition. Oxford Handbooks Online. doi:10.1093/oxfordhb/9780195384253.013.0015

Genesee, F., K. Lindholm-Leary, W., M. Saunders, and D. Christian (eds.). (2006). Educating English Language Learners: A Synthesis of Research Evidence. Cambridge: Cambridge University Press.

Graham, C. (2000). *Jazz Chants Old and New*. 2nd ed. Oxford University Press.

Heath, S.B. (1983). *Ways with Words*. Cambridge: Cambridge University Press.

Krashen, S. (1982). *Principles and Practice in Second Language Acquisition*. Oxford: Pergamon.

Krashen, S. (1989). We acquire vocabulary and spelling by reading: Additional evidence for the input hypothesis. The Modern Language Journal, 73(4), 440-464.

Lambert, W.E. (1997). 'The effects of bilingual and bicultural experiences on children's attitudes and social perspectives' in P. Hornel, M.Palij, and D. Aaronson (eds): *Childhood Bilingualism: Aspects of Linguistic, Cognitive, and Social Development*. Mahwah, NJ: Lawrence Erlbaum and Associates. Pp.197-221.

Lantolf, J.P. (ed.) (2000). *Sociocultural Theory and Second Language Learning*. Oxford: Oxford University Press.

Lindholm-Leary, K. (2001). *Dual Language Education*. Clevedon, UK: Multilingual Matters.

Long, M. (1996). 'The role of the linguistic environment in second language acquisition in W. Ritchie and T. Bhatia (eds.): *Handbook of Second Language Acquisition*. New York: Academic Press. pp. 413-68.

New Kids-Center: Eight Greatest Mysteries of the World. Retrieved from the internet on July 3, 2020. http://www.newkidscenter.com/Greatest-Mysteries-of-the-World.html

Moon, C., Lagercrantz, H., & Kuhl, P. K. (2013). Language experienced in utero affects vowel perception after birth: A two-country study. *Acta Paediatrica, 102*(2), 156-160. doi:10.1111/apa.12098

Operation Meditation: 66 Deep Philosophical Questions. Retrieved from the Internet on July 3, 2020. http://operationmeditation.com/discover/65-deep-philosophical-questions/

Paradis, J., F. Genesee, & M.B. Crago (2011). Dual Language Development and Disorder: A Handbook on Bilingualism and Second Language Learning 2nd edn. Baltimore Paul H. Brookes.

Paul, R.; Elder, L. (2004). *Critical and creative thinking.* Dillon Beach, CA: The Foundation for Critical Thinking.

Perez-Prado, A. (2016). Habits of Mind for homeschooling: A guide for parents and teachers. Westport, CT: Institute for Habits of Mind International.

Perez-Prado, A. (2019). Habits of Mind with English Language Learners. In *Nurturing Habits of Mind in Early Childhood: Success Stories from Around the World.* Costa & Kallick (eds.). Alexandria, VA: ASCD.

Sarem, S. & Shirzadi, Y. (2014). A critical review of the interactionist approach to second language acquisition. Journal of Applied Linguistics and Language Research, 1(1),

Swain, M. Language Teaching. Cambridge Vol. 46, Iss. 2, (Apr 2013): 195-207.DOI:10.1017/S0261444811000486.

Rothstein, D. and Santana, L. (2011) Make Just One Change: Teach Students to Ask Their Own Questions. Harvard Education Press.

Seligman, M. E. P. (2002). *Authentic Happiness: Using the new positive psychology to realize your potential for lasting fulfillment.* New York, U.S.A.: Simon & Schuster, Inc.

Thornburg, D. D. Ph.D. (2010) "Why 'Why' is More Important Than 'What' in Education." Thornburg Center for Space Exploration: http://www.tcse-k12.org/pages/whywhy.pdf.

Appendix

 1. Persisting

Stick to it!
Persevering in task through to completion; remaining focused. Looking for ways to reach your goal when stuck. Not giving up.

 2. Managing Impulsivity

Take your time!

Thinking before acting; remaining calm, thoughtful and deliberative.

 3. Listening with understanding and empathy

Understand others!

Devoting mental energy to another person's thoughts and ideas; Make an effort to perceive another's point of view and emotions.

 4. Thinking flexibly

Look at it another way!

Being able to change perspectives, generate alternatives, consider options.

 5. Thinking about your thinking
(Metacognition)

Know your knowing!

Being aware of your own thoughts, strategies, feelings and actions and their effects on others.

 6. Striving for accuracy

Check it again!

Always doing your best. Setting high standards. Checking and finding ways to improve constantly.

 7. Questioning and problem posing

How do you know?
Having a questioning attitude; knowing what data are needed & developing questioning strategies to produce those data. Finding problems to solve.

 8. Applying past knowledge to new situations

Use what you learn!

Accessing prior knowledge; transferring knowledge beyond the situation in which it was learned.

 9. Thinking & communicating with clarity and precision

Be clear!

Strive for accurate communication in both written and oral form; avoiding over-generalizations, distortions, deletions and exaggerations.

 10. Gather data through all senses

Use your natural pathways!

Pay attention to the world around you Gather data through all the senses. taste, touch, smell, hearing and sight.

 11. Creating, imagining, and innovating

Try a different way!

Generating new and novel ideas, fluency, originality

 12. Responding with wonderment and awe

Have fun figuring it out!

Finding the world awesome, mysterious and being intrigued with phenomena and beauty.

 13. Taking responsible risks

Venture out!

Being adventuresome; living on the edge of one's competence. Try new things constantly.

 14. Finding humor

Laugh a little!

Finding the whimsical, incongruous and unexpected. Being able to laugh at one's self.

 15. Thinking interdependently

Work together!

Being able to work in and learn from others in reciprocal situations. Team work.

 16. Remaining open to continuous learning

Learn from experiences!

Having humility and pride when admitting we don't know; resisting complacency.

Appendix B

HABITS OF MIND

Arthur L. Costa, Ed. D.
Professor Emeritus,
California State University, Sacramento

> Habit is a cable; we weave a thread of it each day, and at last we cannot break it.
> Horace Mann
> American Educator
> 1796-1859

By definition, a problem is any stimulus, question, task, phenomenon, or discrepancy, the explanation for which is not immediately known. Thus, we are interested in focusing on student performance under those challenging conditions that demand strategic reasoning, insightfulness, perseverance, creativity, and craftsmanship to resolve a complex problem. Not only are we interested in how many answers students know, but also in knowing how they behave when they DON'T know. Habits of Mind are performed in response to those questions and problems the answers to which are NOT immediately known. We are interested in observing how students produce knowledge rather than how they merely reproduce knowledge. The critical attribute of intelligent human beings is not only having information, but also knowing how to act on it.

A "Habit of Mind" means having a disposition toward behaving intelligently when confronted with problems. When humans experience dichotomies, are confused by dilemmas, or come face to face with uncertainties--our most effective actions require drawing forth certain patterns of intellectual behavior. When we draw upon these intellectual resources, the results that are produced are more powerful, of higher quality and of greater significance than if we fail to employ those intellectual behaviors.

Employing "Habits of Mind" requires a composite of many skills, attitudes, cues, past experiences and proclivities. It means that we value one pattern of thinking over another and therefore it implies choice making about which pattern should be employed at this time. It includes alertness to the contextual cues that signal this as an appropriate time and circumstance in which the employment of this pattern would be useful. It requires a level of skillfulness to employ and carry through the behaviors effectively over time. It suggests that as a result of each experience in which these behaviors were employed, the effects of their use are reflected upon, evaluated, modified and carried forth to future applications.

HABITS OF MIND ATTEND TO:

• **Value:**	Choosing to employ a pattern of intellectual behaviors rather than other, less productive patterns.
• **Inclination:**	Feeling the tendency toward employing a pattern of intellectual behaviors.
• **Sensitivity:**	Perceiving opportunities for, and appropriateness of employing the pattern of behavior.
• **Capability:**	Possessing the basic skills and capacities to carry through with the behaviors.
• **Commitment:**	Constantly striving to reflect on and improve performance of the pattern of intellectual behavior.

1

DESCRIBING HABITS OF MIND

> When we no longer know what to do we have come to our real work and when we no
> longer know which way to go we have begun our real journey. The mind that is not
> baffled is not employed. The impeded stream is the one that sings.
> Wendell Berry

What behaviors are indicative of the efficient, effective problem solver? Just what do human beings do when they behave intelligently? Research in effective thinking and intelligent behavior by Feuerstein (1980), Glatthorn and Baron (1985), Sternberg (1985), Perkins (1985), Ennis, (1985) and Goleman (1995) indicates that there are some identifiable characteristics of effective thinkers. These are not necessarily scientists, artists, mathematicians or the wealthy who demonstrate these behaviors. These characteristics have been identified in successful mechanics, teachers, entrepreneurs, salespeople, and parents—people in all walks of life.

Following are descriptions and an elaboration of 16 attributes of what human beings do when they behave intelligently. We choose to refer to them as *Habits of Mind.* These habits are seldom performed in isolation. Rather, clusters of such habits are drawn forth and employed in various situations. When listening intently, for example, one employs flexibility, metacognition, precise language and perhaps questioning.

Please do not think that there are only sixteen ways in which humans display their intelligence. This list is not meant to be complete. It should serve to initiate the collection of additional attributes. Although 16 Habits of Mind are described here, you, your colleagues and your students will want to continue the search for additional Habits of Mind by adding to and elaborating on this list and the descriptions.

1. Persisting

> Be like a postage stamp—stick to one thing until you get there.
> Margaret Carty

 Efficacious people stick to a task until it is completed. They don't give up easily. They are able to analyze a problem, to develop a system, structure, or strategy to attack a problem. They employ a range and have repertoire of alternative strategies for problem solving. They collect evidence to indicate their problem-solving strategy is working, and if one strategy doesn't work, they know how to back up and try another. They recognize when a theory or idea must be rejected and another employed. They have systematic methods of analyzing a problem that include knowing how to begin, knowing what steps must be performed, and what data need to be generated or collected. Because they are able to sustain a problem solving process over time, they are comfortable with ambiguous situations.

Students often give up in despair when the answer to a problem is not immediately known. They sometimes crumple their papers and throw them away saying, "I can't do this," "It's too hard," or, they write down any answer to get the task over with as quickly as possible. Some have attention deficits; they have difficulty staying focused for any length of time, they are easily distracted, they lack the ability to analyze a problem, to develop a system, structure, or strategy of problem

204

attack. They may give up because they have a limited repertoire of problem solving strategies. If their strategy doesn't work, they give up because they have no alternatives.

2. Managing Impulsivity

> "....goal directed self-imposed delay of gratification is perhaps the essence of emotional self-regulation: the ability to deny impulse in the service of a goal, whether it be building a business, solving an algebraic equation, or pursuing the Stanley cup.
> Daniel Goleman *Emotional Intelligence* (1995) p. 83

Effective problem solvers have a sense of deliberativeness: They think before they act. They intentionally form a vision of a product, plan of action, goal or a destination before they begin. They strive to clarify and understand directions, develop a strategy for approaching a problem and withhold immediate value judgments before fully understanding an idea. Reflective individuals consider alternatives and consequences of several possible directions prior to taking action. They decrease their need for trial and error by gathering information, taking time to reflect on an answer before giving it, making sure they understand directions, and listening to alternative points of view.

Often students blurt the first answer that comes to mind. Sometimes they shout out an answer, start to work without fully understanding the directions. They lack an organized plan or strategy for approaching a problem. They may take the first suggestion given or operate on the most obvious and simple idea that comes to mind rather than considering more complex alternatives and consequences of several possible directions.

3. Listening To Others—With Understanding and Empathy

> Listening is the beginning of understanding.....
> Wisdom is the reward for a lifetime of listening.
> Let the wise listen and add to their learning and let the discerning get guidance -
> Proverbs 1:5

Highly effective people spend an inordinate amount of time and energy listening (Covey, 1989). Some psychologists believe that the ability to listen to another person, to empathize with, and to understand their point of view is one of the highest forms of intelligent behavior. Being able to paraphrase another person's ideas, detecting indicators (cues) of their feelings or emotional states in their oral and body language (empathy), accurately expressing another person's concepts, emotions and problems—all are indications of listening behavior (Piaget called it "overcoming ego-centrism"). They are able to see through the diverse perspectives of others. They gently attend to another person demonstrating their understanding of and empathy for an idea or feeling by paraphrasing it accurately, building upon it, clarifying it, or giving an example of it.

Senge and his colleagues (1994) suggest that to listen fully means to pay close attention to what is being said beneath the words. You listen not only to the "music", but also to the essence of the person speaking. You listen not only for what someone knows, but also for

3

what he or she is trying to represent. Ears operate at the speed of sound, which is far slower than the speed of light the eyes take in. Generative listening is the art of developing deeper silences in yourself, so you can slow your mind's hearing to your ears' natural speed, and hear beneath the words to their meaning.

We spend 55 percent of our lives listening yet it is one of the least taught skills in schools. We often say we are listening but in actuality, we are rehearsing in our head what we are going to say next when our partner is finished. Some students ridicule, laugh at, or put down other students' ideas. They interrupt are unable to build upon, consider the merits of, or operate on another person's ideas. We want our students to learn to devote their mental energies to another person and invest themselves in their partner's ideas.

We wish students to learn to hold in abeyance their own values, judgments, opinions, and prejudices in order to listen to and entertain another person's thoughts. This is a very complex skill requiring the ability to monitor one's own thoughts while, at the same time, attending to their partner's words. This does not mean that we can't disagree with someone. A good listener tries to understand what the other person is saying. In the end he may disagree sharply, but because he disagrees, he wants to know exactly what it is he is disagreeing with.

4. Thinking Flexibly

> If you never change your mind, why have one?
> Edward deBono

An amazing discovery about the human brain is its plasticity--its ability to "rewire", change and even repair itself to become smarter. Flexible people are the ones with the most control. They have the capacity to change their mind as they receive additional data. They engage in multiple and simultaneous outcomes and activities, draw upon a repertoire of problem solving strategies and can practice style flexibility, knowing when it is appropriate to be broad and global in their thinking and when a situation requires detailed precision. They create and seek novel approaches and have a well-developed sense of humor. They envision a range of consequences.

Flexible people can approach a problem from a new angle using a novel approach {deBono (1970) refers to this as *lateral thinking*.} They consider alternative points of view or deal with several sources of information simultaneously. Their minds are open to change based on additional information and data or reasoning, which contradicts their beliefs. Flexible people know that they have and can develop options and alternatives to consider. They understand mean-ends relationships being able to work within rules, criteria and regulations and they can predict the consequences of flouting them. They understand not only the immediate reactions but are also able to perceive the bigger purposes that such constraints serve. Thus, flexibility of mind is essential for working with social diversity, enabling an individual to recognize the wholeness and distinctness of other people's ways of experiencing and making meaning.

Flexible thinkers are able to shift, at will, through multiple perceptual positions. One perceptual orientation is what Jean Piaget called, *egocentrism*--perceiving from our own point of view. By contrast, *allocentrism* is the position in which we perceive through another persons' orientation. We

4

operate from this second position when we empathize with other's feelings, predict how others are thinking, and anticipate potential misunderstandings.

Another perceptual position is "macro-centric". It is similar to looking down from a balcony at ourselves and our interactions with others. This bird's-eye view is useful for discerning themes and patterns from assortments of information. It is intuitive, holistic and conceptual. Since we often need to solve problems with incomplete information, we need the capacity to perceive general patterns and jump across gaps of incomplete knowledge or when some of the pieces are missing.

Yet another perceptual orientation is micro-centric--examining the individual and sometimes minute parts that make up the whole. This "worm's-eye view", without which science, technology, and any complex enterprise could not function, involves logical analytical computation and searching for causality in methodical steps. It requires attention to detail, precision, and orderly progressions.

Flexible thinkers display confidence in their intuition. They tolerate confusion and ambiguity up to a point, and are willing to let go of a problem trusting their subconscious to continue creative and productive work on it. Flexibility is the cradle of humor, creativity and repertoire. While there are many possible perceptual positions--past, present, future, egocentric, allocentric, macro centric, visual, auditory, kinesthetic--the flexible mind is activated by knowing when to shift perceptual positions.

Some students have difficulty in considering alternative points of view or dealing with more than one classification system simultaneously. THEIR way to solve a problem seems to be the ONLY way. They perceive situations from a very ego-centered point of view: "My way or the highway!" Their mind is made up; "Don't confuse me with facts, that's it."

5. Thinking About our Thinking (Metacognition)

> When the mind is thinking it is talking to itself
> Plato

 Occurring in the neocortex, metacognition is our ability to know what we know and what we don't know. It is our ability to plan a strategy for producing what information is needed, to be conscious of our own steps and strategies during the act of problem solving, and to reflect on and evaluate the productiveness of our own thinking. While "inner language," thought to be a prerequisite, begins in most children around age five, metacognition is a key attribute of formal thought flowering about age eleven.

Probably the major components of metacognition are developing a plan of action, maintaining that plan in mind over a period of time, then reflecting back on and evaluating the plan upon its completion. Planning a strategy before embarking on a course of action assists us in keeping track of the steps in the sequence of planned behavior at the conscious awareness level for the duration of the activity. It facilitates making temporal and comparative judgments, assessing the readiness for more or different activities, and monitoring our interpretations, perceptions, decisions and behaviors. An example of this would be what superior teachers do daily: developing a teaching strategy for a lesson, keeping that strategy in mind throughout the instruction, then reflecting back upon the strategy to evaluate its effectiveness in producing the desired student outcomes.

5

Intelligent people plan for, reflect on, and evaluate the quality of their own thinking skills and strategies. Metacognition means becoming increasingly aware of one's actions and the effect of those actions on others and on the environment; forming internal questions as one searches for information and meaning, developing mental maps or plans of action, mentally rehearsing prior to performance, monitoring those plans as they are employed--being conscious of the need for midcourse correction if the plan is not meeting expectations, reflecting on the plan upon completion of the implementation for the purpose of self-evaluation, and editing mental pictures for improved performance.

Interestingly, not all humans achieve the level of formal operations (Chiabetta, 1976). And as Alexander Luria, the Russian psychologist found, not all adults metacogitate (Whimbey, 1976). The most likely reason is that we do not take the time to reflect on our experiences. Students often do not take the time to wonder why we are doing what we are doing. They seldom question themselves about their own learning strategies or evaluate the efficiency of their own performance. Some children virtually have no idea of what they should do when they confront a problem and are often unable to explain their strategies of decision making (Sternberg and Wagner, 1982). When teachers ask, "How did you solve that problem; what strategies did you have in mind"? or, "Tell us what went on in your head to come up with that conclusion". Students often respond by saying, "I don't know, I just did it.'

We want our students to perform well on complex cognitive tasks. A simple example of this might be drawn from a reading task. It is a common experience while reading a passage to have our minds "wander" from the pages. We "see" the words but no meaning is being produced. Suddenly we realize that we are not concentrating and that we've lost contact with the meaning of the text. We "recover" by returning to the passage to find our place, matching it with the last thought we can remember, and, once having found it, reading on with connectedness. This inner awareness and the strategy of recovery are components of metacognition.

6. Striving For Accuracy and Precision

> A man who has committed a mistake and doesn't correct it
> is committing another mistake.
> Confucius

Embodied in the stamina, grace and elegance of a ballerina or a shoemaker, is the desire for craftsmanship, mastery, flawlessness and economy of energy to produce exceptional results. People who value accuracy, precision and craftsmanship take time to check over their products. They review the rules by which they are to abide; they review the models and visions they are to follow; and they review the criteria they are to employ and confirm that their finished product matches the criteria exactly. To be craftsmanlike means knowing that one can continually perfect one's craft by working to attain the highest possible standards, and pursue ongoing learning in order to bring a laser like focus of energies to task accomplishment. These people take pride in their work and have a desire for accuracy as they take time to check over their work. Craftsmanship includes exactness, precision, accuracy, correctness, faithfulness, and fidelity. For some people, craftsmanship requires continuous reworking. Mario Cuomo, a great speechwriter and politician, once said that his speeches were never done—it was only a deadline that made him stop working on them!

6

208

Some students may turn in sloppy, incomplete or uncorrected work. They are more anxious to get rid of the assignment than to check it over for accuracy and precision. They are willing to suffice with minimum effort rather than investing their maximum. They may be more interested in expedience rather than excellence.

7. Questioning and Posing Problems

> The formulation of a problem is often more essential than its solution, which may be merely a matter of mathematical or experimental skill.
> To raise new questions, a new possibility, to regard old problems from a new angle, requires creative imagination and marks real advances.....
> Albert Einstein

One of the distinguishing characteristics between humans and other forms of life is our inclination, and ability to FIND problems to solve. Effective problem solvers know how to ask questions to fill in the gaps between what they know and what they don't know. Effective questioners are inclined to ask a range of questions. For example: requests for data to support others' conclusions and assumptions—such questions as,

"What evidence do you have.....?"
"How do you know that's true?"
"How reliable is this data source?"

They pose questions about alternative points of view:

"From whose viewpoint are we seeing, reading of hearing?"
"From what angle, what perspective are we viewing this situation?"

Students pose questions, which make causal connections and relationships:

"How are these people (events) (situations) related to each other?"
"What produced this connection?"

They pose hypothetical problems characterized by "iffy"-type questions:

"What do you think would happen IF.....?"
"IF that is true, then what might happen if....?"

Inquirers recognize discrepancies and phenomena in their environment and probe into their causes: "Why do cats purr?" "How high can birds fly?" "Why does the hair on my head grow so fast, while the hair on my arms and legs grows so slowly? "What would happen if we put the saltwater fish in a fresh water aquarium?" "What are some alternative solutions to international conflicts other than wars?"

Some students may be unaware of the functions, classes, syntax or intentions in questions. They may not realize that questions vary in complexity, structure and purpose. They may pose simple questions intending to derive maximal results. When confronted with a discrepancy, they may lack an overall strategy of search and solution finding.

7

8. Applying Past Knowledge to New Situations

> "I've never made a mistake. I've only learned from experience."
> Thomas A. Edison

Intelligent human beings learn from experience. When confronted with a new and perplexing problem they will often draw forth experience from their past. They can often be heard to say, "This reminds me of...." or "This is just like the time when I..." They explain what they are doing now in terms of analogies with or references to previous experiences. They call upon their store of knowledge and experience as sources of data to support theories to explain, or processes to solve each new challenge. Furthermore, they are able to abstract meaning from one experience, carry it forth, and apply it in a new and novel situation.

Too often students begin each new task as if it were being approached for the very first time. Teachers are often dismayed when they invite students to recall how they solved a similar problem previously and students don't remember. It's as if they never heard of it before, even though they had the same type of problem just recently. It is as if each experience is encapsulated and has no relationship to what has come before or what comes afterward. Their thinking is what psychologists refer to as an "episodic grasp of reality" (Feuerstein 1980). That is, each event in life is a separate and discrete event with no connections to what may have come before or with no relation to what follows. Furthermore, their learning is so encapsulated that they seem unable to draw forth from one event and apply it in another context.

9. Thinking and Communicating with Clarity and Precision

> "The limits of my language are the limits of my mind. All I know is what I have words for."
> Ludwig Wittgenstein

Language refinement plays a critical role in enhancing a person's cognitive maps and their ability to think critically which is the knowledge base for efficacious action. Enriching the complexity and specificity of language simultaneously produces effective thinking.

Language and thinking are closely entwined. Like either side of a coin, they are inseparable. When you hear fuzzy language, it is a reflection of fuzzy thinking. Intelligent people strive to communicate accurately in both written and oral form taking care to use precise language, defining terms, using correct names and universal labels and analogies. They strive to avoid overgeneralizations, deletions and distortions. Instead they support their statements with explanations, comparisons, quantification, and evidence.

We sometimes hear students and other adults using vague and imprecise language. They describe objects or events with words like *weird, nice,* or *OK*. They call specific objects using such non-descriptive words as *stuff, junk* and *things*. They punctuate sentences with meaningless interjections like *ya know, er* and *uh*. They use vague or general nouns and pronouns: "*They* told me to do it". "*Everybody* has one." "*Teachers* don't understand me. They use non-specific verbs: "Let's *do* it." and unqualified comparatives: "This soda is *better,* I like it *more*".

8

10. Gathering Data through All Senses

The brain is the ultimate reductionist. It reduces the world to its elementary parts: photons of light, molecules of smell, sound waves, vibrations of touch--which send electrochemical signals to individual brain cells that store information about lines, movements, colors, smells and other sensory inputs.

Many scientists say we actually have nine senses: External senses that are engaged from external sources include sight, sound, taste, touch, and smell. They provide information about the outside world. Pain, balance, thirst and hunger are considered to be our internal senses. They provide information about the body and its needs. For example, the sense of hunger shows that the body needs food.

Intelligent people know that all information gets into the brain through these sensory pathways: gustatory, olfactory, tactile, kinesthetic, auditory, visual, Most linguistic, cultural, and physical learning is derived from the environment by observing or taking in through the senses. To know a wine it must be drunk; to know a role it must be acted; to know a game it must be played; to know a dance it must be moved; to know a goal it must be envisioned. Those whose sensory pathways are open, alert, and acute absorb more information from the environment than those whose pathways are withered, immune, and oblivious to sensory stimuli do.

Furthermore, we are learning more about the impact of arts and music on improved mental functioning. Forming mental images is important in mathematics and engineering; listening to classical music seems to improve spatial reasoning.

Social scientists solve problems through scenarios and role-playing; scientists build models; engineers use cad-cam; mechanics learn through hands-on experimentation; artists experiment with colors and textures. Musicians experiment by producing combinations of instrumental and vocal music.

Some students, however, go through school and life oblivious to the textures, rhythms, patterns sounds and colors around them. Sometimes children are afraid to touch, get their hands "dirty" or feel some object might be "slimy" or "icky". They operate within a narrow range of sensory problem solving strategies wanting only to "describe it but not illustrate or act it", or "listen but not participate". To insure powerful learning, we want students to experience the world through as many different avenues as possible.

11. Creating, Imagining, and Innovating

9

All human beings have the capacity to generate novel, original, clever or ingenious products, solutions, and techniques—if that capacity is developed. Creative human beings try to conceive problem solutions differently, examining alternative possibilities from many angles. They tend to project themselves into different roles using analogies, starting with a vision and working backward, imagining they are the objects being considered. Creative people take risks and frequently push the boundaries of their perceived limits (Perkins 1985). They are intrinsically rather than extrinsically motivated, working on the task because of the aesthetic challenge rather than the material rewards. Creative people are open to criticism. They hold up their products for others to judge and seek feedback in an ever-increasing effort to refine their technique. They are uneasy with the status quo. They constantly strive for greater fluency, elaboration, novelty, parsimony, simplicity, craftsmanship, perfection, beauty, harmony, and balance.

Students, however, are often heard saying, "I can't draw," "I was never very good at art," "I can't sing a note," "I'm not creative". Some people believe creative humans are just born that way; it's in their genes and chromosomes.

12. Responding with Wonderment and Awe

The most beautiful experience in the world is the experience of the mysterious."
Albert Einstein.

Describing the 200 best and brightest of the All USA College Academic Team identified by USA Today, Tracey Wong Briggs (1999) states, "They are creative thinkers who have a passion for what they do." Efficacious people have not only an "I CAN" attitude, but also an "I ENJOY" feeling. They seek problems to solve for themselves and to submit to others. They delight in making up problems to solve on their own and request enigmas from others. They enjoy figuring things out by themselves, and continue to learn throughout their lifetimes.

Some children and adults avoid problems and are "turned off" to learning. They make such comments as, "I was never good at these brain teasers," or "Go ask your father; he's the brain in this family. "Its boring." "When am I ever going to use this stuff?" "Who cares?" "Lighten up, teacher, thinking is hard work," or "I don't do thinking!" Many people never enrolled in another math class or other "hard" academic subjects after they didn't have to in high school or college. Many people perceive thinking as hard work and therefore recoil from situations, which demand "too much" of it.

We want our students, however to be curious; to commune with the world around them; to reflect on the changing formations of a cloud; feel charmed by the opening of a bud; sense the logical simplicity of mathematical order. Students can find beauty in a sunset, intrigue in the geometrics of a spider web, and exhilaration at the iridescence of a hummingbird's wings. They see the congruity and intricacies in the derivation of a mathematical formula, recognize the orderliness and adroitness of a chemical change, and commune with the serenity of a distant constellation. We want them feel compelled, enthusiastic and passionate about learning, inquiring and mastering.

10

212

13. Taking Responsible Risks.

> There has been a calculated risk in every stage of American development--the pioneers who were not afraid of the wilderness, businessmen who were not afraid of failure, dreamers who were not afraid of action.
> Brooks Atkinson

Flexible people seem to have an almost uncontrollable urge to go beyond established limits. They are uneasy about comfort; they "live on the edge of their competence". They seem compelled to place themselves in situations where they do not know what the outcome will be. They accept confusion, uncertainty, and the higher risks of failure as part of the normal process and they learn to view setbacks as interesting, challenging and growth producing. However, they are not behaving impulsively.

Their risks are educated. They draw on past knowledge, are thoughtful about consequences and have a well-trained sense of what is appropriate. They know that all risks are not worth taking!

Risk taking can be considered in two categories: those who see it as a venture and those who see it as adventure. The venture part of risk taking might be described by the venture capitalist. When a person is approached to take the risk of investing in a new business, she will look at the markets, see how well organized the ideas are, and study the economic projections. If she finally decides to take the risk, it is a well-considered one.

The adventure part of risk taking might be described by the experiences from project adventure. In this situation, there is spontaneity, a willingness to take a chance in the moment. Once again, a person will only take the chance if they know that there is either past history that suggests that what they are doing is not going to be life threatening or if they believe that there is enough support in the group to protect them from harm. Ultimately, the learning from such high-risk experiences is that people are far more able to take actions than they previously believed.

It is only through repeated experiences that risk taking becomes educated. It often is a cross between intuition, drawing on past knowledge and a sense of meeting new challenges.
Bobby Jindal, Governor of Louisiana states,

"The only way to succeed is to be brave enough to risk failure. " (Briggs, 1999 p 2A)

When someone holds back from taking risks, he is confronted constantly with missed opportunities. Some students seem reluctant to take risks. Some students hold back games, new learning, and new friendships because their fear of failure is far greater than their experience of venture or adventure. They are reinforced by the mental voice that says, " if you don't try it, you won't be wrong" or "if you try it and you are wrong, you will look stupid". The other voice that might say, "if you don't try it, you will never know" is trapped in fear and mistrust. They are more interested in knowing whether their answer is correct or not, rather than being challenged by the process of finding the answer. They are unable to sustain a process of problem solving and finding the answer over time, and therefore avoid ambiguous situations. They have a need for certainty rather than an inclination for doubt.

11

213

We hope that students will learn how to take intellectual as well as physical risks. Students who are capable of being different, going against the grain of the common, thinking of new ideas and testing them with peers as well as teachers, are more likely to be successful in an era of innovation and uncertainty.

14. Finding Humor

"People who laugh actually live longer than those who don't laugh. Few persons realize that health actually varies according to the amount of laughter."
James J. Walsh

Another unique attribute of human beings is our sense of humor. Laughter transcends all human beings. Its' positive effects on psychological functions include a drop in the pulse rate, the secretion of endorphins, an increased oxygen in the blood. It has been found to liberate creativity and provoke such higher level thinking skills as anticipation, finding novel relationships, visual imagery, and making analogies. People who engage in the mystery of humor have the ability to perceive situations from original and often interesting vantage points. They tend to initiate humor more often, to place greater value on having a sense of humor, to appreciate and understand others' humor and to be verbally playful when interacting with others. Having a whimsical frame of mind, they thrive on finding incongruity and perceiving absurdities, ironies and satire; finding discontinuities and being able to laugh at situations and themselves. Some students find humor in all the "wrong places"--human differences, ineptitude, injurious behavior, vulgarity, violence and profanity. They laugh at others yet are unable to laugh at themselves.

We want our students to acquire the characteristic of creative problem solvers, they can distinguish between situations of human frailty and fallibility that are in need of compassion and those that are truly funny (Dyer, 1997).

15. Thinking Interdependently

Take care of each other. Share your energies with the group. No one must feel alone, cut off, for that is when you do not make it.
Willie Unsoeld
Renowned Mountain Climber

Human beings are social beings. We congregate in groups, find it therapeutic to be listened to, draw energy from one another, and seek reciprocity. In groups we contribute our time and energy to tasks that we would quickly tire of when working alone. In fact, we have learned that one of the cruelest forms of punishment that can be inflicted on an individual is solitary confinement.

Cooperative humans realize that all of us together are more powerful, intellectually and/or physically, than any one individual. Probably the foremost disposition in the post industrial society is the heightened ability to think in concert with others; to find ourselves increasingly more interdependent and sensitive to the needs of others. Problem solving has become so complex that no one person can go it alone. No one has access to all the data needed to make critical decisions; no one person can consider as many alternatives as several people can.

Some students may not have learned to work in groups; they have underdeveloped social skills. They feel isolated; they prefer their solitude. "Leave me alone--I'll do it by my self". " They just don't like me". "I want to be alone." Some students seem unable to contribute to group work either by being a "job hog" or conversely, letting others do all the work.

Working in groups requires the ability to justify ideas and to test the feasibility of solution strategies on others. It also requires the development of a willingness and openness to accept the feedback from a critical friend. Through this interaction the group and the individual continue to grow. Listening, consensus seeking, giving up an idea to work with someone else's, empathy, compassion, group leadership, knowing how to support group efforts, altruism--all are behaviors indicative of cooperative human beings.

16. Learning Continuously

> Insanity is continuing to do the same thing over and over and expecting different results.
> Albert Einstein

Intelligent people are in a continuous learning mode. Their confidence, in combination with their inquisitiveness, allows them to constantly search for new and better ways. People with this Habit of Mind are always striving for improvement, always growing, always learning, always modifying and improving themselves. They seize problems, situations, tensions, conflicts and circumstances as valuable opportunities to learn.

A great mystery about humans is that we confront learning opportunities with fear rather than mystery and wonder. We seem to feel better when we know rather than when we learn. We defend our biases, beliefs, and storehouses of knowledge rather than inviting the unknown, the creative and the inspirational. Being certain and closed gives us comfort while being doubtful and open gives us fear.

From an early age, employing a curriculum of fragmentation, competition and reactiveness, students are trained to believe that deep learning means figuring out the truth rather than developing capabilities for effective and thoughtful action. They have been taught to value certainty rather than doubt, to give answers rather than to inquire, to know which choice is correct rather than to explore alternatives.

Our wish is for creative students and people who are eager to learn. That includes the humility of knowing that we don't know, which is the highest form of thinking we will ever learn. Paradoxically, unless you start off with humility you will never get anywhere, so as the first step you have to have already what will eventually be the crowning glory of all learning: the humility to know--and admit-- that you don't know and not be afraid to find out.

IN SUMMARY

Drawn from research on human effectiveness, descriptions of remarkable performers, and analyses of the characteristics of efficacious people, we have presented descriptions of sixteen Habits of Mind. This list is not meant to be complete but rather to serve as a starting point for further elaboration and description.

13

These Habits of Mind may serve as mental disciplines. When confronted with problematic situations, students, parents and teachers might habitually employ one or more of these Habits of Mind by asking themselves, "What is the most *intelligent thing* I can do right now?"

- How can I learn from this, what are my resources, how can I draw on my past successes with problems like this, what do I already know about the problem, what resources do I have available or need to generate?
- How can I approach this problem *flexibly*? How might I look at the situation in another way, how can I draw upon my repertoire of problem solving strategies; how can I look at this problem from a fresh perspective (Lateral Thinking).
- How can I illuminate this problem to make it clearer, more precise? Do I need to check out my data sources? How might I break this problem down into its component parts and develop a strategy for understanding and accomplishing each step.
- What do I know or not know; what questions do I need to ask, what strategies are in my mind now, what am I aware of in terms of my own beliefs, values and goals with this problem. What feelings or emotions am I aware of which might be blocking or enhancing my progress?
- The interdependent thinker might turn to others for help. They might ask how this problem affects others; how can we solve it together and what can I learn from others that would help me become a better problem solver?

Taking a reflective stance in the midst of active problem solving is often difficult. For that reason, each of these Habits of Mind is situational and transitory. There is no such thing as perfect realization of any of them. They are utopian states toward which we constantly aspire. Csikszentmihalyi (1993, p. 23) states,

> "Although every human brain is able to generate self-reflective consciousness, not everyone seems to use it equally."

Few people, notes Kegan (1994) ever <u>fully</u> reach the stage of cognitive complexity, and rarely before middle age.

These Habits of Mind transcend all subject matters commonly taught in school. They are characteristic of peak performers whether they are in homes, schools, athletic fields, organizations, the military, governments, churches or corporations. They are what make marriages successful, learning continual, workplaces productive and democracies enduring.

The goal of education therefore, should be to support others and ourselves in liberating, developing and habituating these Habits of Mind more fully. Taken together, they are a force directing us toward increasingly authentic, congruent, ethical behavior, the touchstones of integrity. They are the tools of disciplined choice making. They are the primary vehicles in the lifelong journey toward integration. They are the "right stuff" that makes human beings efficacious.

> "We are what we repeatedly do. Excellence, then, is not an act but a habit."
>
> Aristotle

216

REFERENCES

Briggs, Tracey, W. Passion for What They Do Keeps Alumni On First Team. *U. S. A Today.* February 25, 1999. Vol. 17, No. 115 pp. 1A-2A.

Chiabetta, E. L. A. Review Of Piagetian Studies Relevant to Science Instruction at the Secondary and College Levels. *Science Education.* 60. pp. 253-261.

Costa, A. (1991) The Search For Intelligent Life. In A. Costa, (Ed.) *Developing Minds: A Resource Book for Teaching Thinking:* pp. 100-106 Alexandria, VA: Association for Supervision and Curriculum Development.

Csikszentmihalyi, M. (1993). *The Evolving Self: A Psychology for the Third Millennium.* New York, NY: Harper Collins Publishers, Inc.

Covey, S. (1989) *The Seven Habits Of Highly Effective People.* New York: Simon and Schuster.

DeBono, E. (1991) The Cort Thinking Program in A. Costa (Ed) *Developing Minds: Programs for Teaching Thinking.* Alexandria, VA pp. 27-32: Association for Supervision and Curriculum Development.

Dyer, J. (1997) Humor As Process in A. Costa, A and R. Liebmann, (Eds.) *Envisioning Process as Content: Toward a Renaissance Curriculum* pp. 211-229 Thousand Oaks, CA: Corwin Press.

Ennis, R. (1985). Goals for A Critical Thinking Curriculum. In A. L. Costa (Ed.), *Developing Minds: A Resource Book for Teaching Thinking.* Alexandria, VA: Association for Supervision and Curriculum Development, 1985.

Feuerstein, R. Rand, Y.M, Hoffman, M. B., & Miller, R. (1980). *Instrumental Enrichment: An Intervention Program for Cognitive Modifiability.* Baltimore: University Park Press.

Glatthorn, A. & Baron, J. (1985). The Good Thinker. In A. L. Costa (Ed.), *Developing Minds: A Resource Book for Teaching Thinking.* Alexandria, VA: Association for Supervision and Curriculum Development.

Goleman, D. (1995) *Emotional Intelligence: Why It Can Matter More Than I. Q.* New York: Bantam Books.

Kegan, R. (1994) *In Over Our Heads: The Mental Complexity of Modern Life.* Cambridge, Ma: Harvard University Press.

Perkins, D. (1985). What Creative Thinking Is. In A. L. Costa (Ed.), *developing minds: A resource book for teaching thinking.* pp. 85-88 Alexandria, VA: Association for Supervision and Curriculum Development.

Perkins, D. (1995) Outsmarting *I. Q.: The Emerging Science of Learnable Intelligence.* New York: The Free Press.

Senge, P., Ross, R., Smith, B., Roberts, C., & Kleiner, A. (1994) *The Fifth Discipline Fieldbook: Strategies and Tools for Building A Learning Organization.* New York: Doubleday/Currency.

Sternberg, R. and Wagner, R. (1982) Understanding Intelligence: What's In It for Education? Paper submitted to the National Commission on Excellence in Education.

Sternberg, R. (1984). *Beyond I.Q.: A Triarchic Theory of Human Intelligence.* New York: Cambridge University Press.

Sternberg, R. (1983) *How Can We Teach Intelligence?* Philadelphia, PA: Research for Better Schools

Whimbey, A. and Whimbey L. S. (1975) *Intelligence Can Be Taught.* New York: Lawrence Erlbaum Associates.

This article is adapted from Costa, A and Kallick, B (2009) *Learning and Leading* with *Habits of Mind: 16 Characteristics for Success.* Alexandria, VA: Association for Supervision and Curriculum Development.

15

HABITS OF MIND

Habits of Mind are dispositions displayed by intelligent people in response to problems, dilemmas, and enigmas, the resolution of which are not immediately apparent.

1. Persisting: *Stick to it!* Persevering in task through to completion; remaining focused	**2. Managing impulsivity:** *Take your Time!* Thinking before acting; remaining calm thoughtful and deliberative.
3. Listening with understanding and empathy: Understand *Others!* Devoting mental energy to another person's thoughts and ideas; holding in abeyance one's own thoughts in order to perceive another's point of view and emotions	**4. Thinking flexibly:** *Look at it Another Way!* Being able to change perspectives, generate alternatives, consider options.
5. Thinking about your Thinking (Metacognition): *Know your knowing!* Being aware of one's own thoughts, strategies, feelings and actions and their effects on others.	**6. Striving for accuracy and precision:** *Check it again!* A desire for exactness, fidelity and craftsmanship.
7. Questioning and Problem Posing: How *do you know?* Having a questioning attitude; knowing what data are needed and developing questioning strategies to produce those data. Finding problems to solve.	**8. Applying past knowledge to new situations.** *Use what you Learn!* Accessing prior knowledge; transferring knowledge beyond the situation in which it was learned.
9. Thinking and Communicating with clarity and Precision: *Be clear!* Striving for accurate communication in both written and oral form; avoiding over generalizations, distortions and deletions	**10. Gathering Data Through all Senses:** *Use your natural pathways!* Gathering data through all the sensory pathways--gustatory, olfactory, tactile, kinesthetic, auditory and visual.
11. Creating, imagining, and innovating *Try a different way!* Generating new and novel ideas, fluency, originality	**12. Responding with Wonderment and awe:** *Have fun figuring it out!* Finding the world awesome, mysterious and being intrigued with phenomena and beauty.
13. Taking Responsible Risks: *Venture out!* Being adventuresome; living on the edge of one's competence	**14. Finding Humor:** Laugh *a little!* Finding the whimsical, incongruous and unexpected. Being able to laugh at oneself.
15. Thinking Interdependently: *Work together!* Being able to work in and learn from others in reciprocal situations.	**16. Remaining Open to Continuous Learning:** Learn *from experiences!* Having humility and pride when admitting we don't know; resisting complacency.

16